The Cocktail Garnish Manual

THE COCKTAIL GARNISH MANUAL

The complete guide to cocktail garnishes
from simple to extraordinary

PHILIPPE TULULA

New World Cocktail Publishing

ISBN: 13: 978-0692507001

CONTENTS

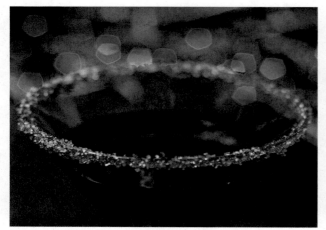

Preface

"Boy, what a day! I need a drink!" exclaims Jim, waving goodnight to his assistant Bonny. "Enjoy!", says Bonny as Jim steps into the elevator. Walking down the street on this sweltering Georgia summer night, Jim has only one thing on his mind: a stiff but refreshing drink. He notices across the street a new bar that he had not visited before. He crosses the road, walks in and sits at the bar.

The decor is faux-prohibition with plenty of dark red velvet and polished brass, and a cozy yet impersonal atmosphere. He is greeted (if you count a barely perceptible nod as a greeting) by the bartender donning a white starched shirt, a sleeve garter and a waxed handlebar mustache.

"What'll it be?" asks the bartender, not even looking in Jim's direction. Exhausted by the hard day at work, Jim just wants something simple. "Gin & Tonic, please", he announces.

The mustachioed bartender looks up at Jim briefly, rolls his eyes and picks up a rocks glass from the rack. A scoop of crystal-clear ice cubes, a shot of Tanqueray, a healthy helping of what looks like homemade tonic water, a quick whirl, and the drink is unceremoniously presented to Jim.

"Umm... excuse me", says Jim sheepishly, "could I have a wedge of lime?". "Sorry, we don't do garnishes here", curtly retorts the barman, with an exasperated sigh and another roll of the eyes. Baffled and a bit insulted, Jim wants to confront the obnoxious barkeeper on this stance, but since he does not have the energy for such a debate and realizing the futility of the discussion, he stops mid-sentence and just silently downs his G&T, pays and leaves (never to return to this bar again).

The preceding scene, though dramatized for effect, is symbolic of the current polemic over garnishes. It's hard to imagine that something as innocuous as a measly lime wedge or a lemon twist could be so controversial. Yet, in the cocktail world, garnishes generate religious-war-like debates only surpassed by how-dry-should-a-martini-be pissing contests.

Adopting an alleged minimalist approach, some argue that garnishes are superfluous, that what matters is the liquid in the glass, and everything else just gets in the way. Some bartenders think it's a waste of their time, especially during a busy night. Never mind that most guests do enjoy and expect garnishes (especially women), these barkeepers can't be bothered. In my opinion, they are missing the point of any hospitality business: delighting your guests.

Others adopt a more balanced approach, only using a garnish if it adds something to the taste of the libation.

Finally, some consider the garnish an integral part of the drink, adding visual appeal or flavor and often both.

For years, chefs have understood the importance of the aesthetic aspects of a dish. All modern chefs have stepped up their game to create dishes that are a feast for the eyes, with elaborate presentations that can be dramatic, daring and sometimes whimsical. Studies have shown that dishes that are appreciated first visually will always taste better to the consumer. It's a psychological effect that is well documented and put to good use by the kitchen greats such as Ferran Adria, Heston Blumenthal and Grant Achatz.

But sadly, the cocktail world is still lagging in that department. Even though great strides have been made in recent years in enhancing the sophistication of the flavor profiles, as well as improving the quality of the ingredients, the visual part of the drink has not been a focus yet in most bars.

As you probably surmised from the preceding diatribe – and from the fact I wrote an entire book on the subject – I sit firmly in the camp of those who see the garnish as an integral part of the cocktail experience.

That being said, I am not advocating just tossing any ole chunk o' fruit on top of a drink. It's true that a lot of garnishes found in your average bar have historically been terrible: from the infamous bright-red maraschino cherry to the brownish wedge of lime that has been sitting in a gloopy room-temperature container for a week. But let's not throw away the baby with the soda water. Just because garnishes have historically been of poor quality does not mean we should forgo them altogether. No, I'm a firm believer in using high-quality produce to garnish drinks and a fervent advocate of creativity in this department.

Garnishes are, in my opinion, the next frontier of this cocktail renaissance we're experiencing and, through this book, I hope to inspire you to join me in that quest and to step up your garnish game.

Introduction

WHO IS THIS BOOK FOR?

This book is for everybody who has an interest in improving their cocktail garnishes. It caters to all skill levels and experiences: from beginner to professional. I do not make any assumption on your knowledge and start from scratch describing items as simple as a citrus wedge or wheel. From then, we build up with variations on the classics and end with some advanced and even crazy garnishes inspired by the modernist movement.

That being said, all garnishes presented here, even the most advanced one, are well within reach of the home enthusiast and do not require any esoteric or expensive equipment to produce. The only requirement is a little patience and practice.

A note on terminology: throughout the book, I refer to the "bartender" and the "guest". I use these words generically and do not imply a professional bar context. The "bartender" could just be a cocktail enthusiast making a drink at home, and the "guest" may be his/her spouse or a friend.

HOW THIS BOOK IS ORGANIZED

The first section of the book contains a general introduction to garnishes, including a brief history, reasons for the importance of garnishes, a description of essential garnishing tools, tips on producing quality garnishes, guidelines for choosing the right garnish and other general tips.

The rest of the book is organized by type of garnish with techniques ranging from basic to complex. For each garnish, I will give general tips as well as step-by-step instructions with detailed pictures.

I tried to cover every form of garnish, sometimes stretching the definition of the word to include rims, specialty ice, use of fire and modernist techniques. But do not think of this book as the be-all and end-all. Rather, treat it as a source of inspiration. Garnishing is an art form, and like all art forms, it is only limited by your imagination. So, feel free to adapt any of the garnishes presented here and create your own.

Here's an overview of each chapter.

Chapter 1 – Citrus. This is the largest chapter since citrus is the most common item used in garnishes. We start with simple wedges, swaths and wheels, then we move on to more advanced variations and finally describe more challenging but very impressive citrus garnishes.

Chapter 2 – Cherries & Berries. This chapter covers two popular categories of red fruit: cherries and berries. We discuss not only the use of cherries in garnishes but also tips on buying and making quality Maraschino cherries. As for berries, we look at strawberries, lychees and blueberries. We also discuss cobblers.

Chapter 3 – Apples. Starting with basic apple wedges and slices, we quickly progress to more interesting garnishes such as fans and offset wedges.

Chapter 4 – Other Fruits. This chapter discusses fruits less commonly used in garnishes. In particular, we cover pineapples, bananas, coconuts, melons, star fruits, kumquats and kiwis.

Chapter 5 – Multi-fruit Garnishes. Here, we discuss garnishes made of a combination of different types of fruit. We cover skewers, flags, boats and variations thereof, as well as more challenging garnishes.

Chapter 6 – Savory Garnishes. This chapter is dedicated to savory garnishes. We start with olives and onions, before moving on to garnishes made of cucumber, celery, carrots, as well as the use of herbs, spices, flowers, bacon and jerky. We end with a discussion of insane Bloody Mary garnishes.

Chapter 7 – Rims. This section covers techniques used to rim a glass. We discuss the "edge" and the "band" and go over tips and ideas for selecting rimming ingredients.

Chapter 8 – Fire and Ice. This chapter covers the use of fire (as in flaming twists or floating flames) and ice (with tips on how to jazz up ice cubes, as well as other ice-related tricks).

Chapter 9 – Sugar Work. Here, we discuss various ways to use sugar in cocktail garnishes. We first cover proper camarelization techniques and apply them to create decorations inspired by the pastry world. We also go over the use of cotton candy and meringues, and learn how to candy and caramelize fruit.

Chapter 10 – Chocolate. This chapter shows you how to temper chocolate and use it in a variety of garnishes. In particular, we discuss shavings, piping, cutouts, shards, curls, cages, spirals, rims and truffles.

Chapter 11 – Modernist Techniques. Here, we discuss how to apply modernist and molecular gastronomy techniques to the cocktail garnish. We cover spherification, foams, powdered cocktails and smoke.

Chapter 12 – Miscellaneous Garnishes. This chapter covers a number of techniques that did not fit cleanly in any other chapter, such as patterns, dehydrated fruits, container garnishes and inedible garnishes.

WHY GARNISH?

Garnishes are more than a visual gratuitous afterthought. In my mind, they are as much a part of the drink as the ingredients in it, and as such, a garnish should be chosen to complement the drink in taste, smell and appearance. Indeed, though sometimes purely visual, garnishes usually affect the taste of the drink by bringing a little sourness, bitterness, or an undefinable nuance to the drink.

This is especially important when the garnish introduces an aroma to the mix, as for instance when one squeezes the oils from a citrus peel over a drink. We know that most of what we perceive as taste is from the aroma (i.e. the smell). So the lack of a garnish may result in not only a less visually appealing product, but also one that lacks crucial depth. The same goes for adding an olive to a Martini or an onion to a Gibson; they not only give the drink a classy look, but add a savory note that complements perfectly the gin and vermouth's botanical flavors.

Another good example is the use of spices (e.g. cinnamon or nutmeg) sprinkled on the surface of the drink. The aroma emitted by the spice will add another dimension to the drink as the guest lifts the glass to his/her mouth. The spices can be placed in a pattern enhancing the visual presentation as well (chapter 12).

Some garnishes are indeed purely visual (that pretty umbrella on the side of your tiki drink will not contribute much flavor...). But I would argue they are the minority. In general, one should be choosing a garnish based on the main flavors of the drink and provide a good pairing.

Finally, garnishes can also act as an indication or reminder for the guest of what flavor is in the drink.

BRIEF HISTORY

Most of cocktail history is unknown, vague, anecdotal or apocryphal. This is hardly surprising; how much do you remember after a night of heavy drinking? So, it is to be expected that the recorded history of mixed alcoholic beverages be a little...um... blurry.

The history of garnishes is no exception to this uncertainty principle. Jerry Thomas' 1862 *The Bon Vivant's Companion* (the first authoritative book on mixed drinks) references citrus peels as garnishes without referring to them as a novel idea, so we know it was common practice at least this far back. He also instructed to "dress" or "ornament the top with fresh fruit".

Juleps (with their large bunch of mint) and Cobblers (with generous toppings of fresh fruits) also represent two categories of heavily garnished drinks popular throughout the 19th century.

But, it is not clear, for instance, at what point the olive became the standard garnish for a Martini and the onion for a Gibson.

As you see, it is impossible to give adequate credit to the creator of any specific garnish. Techniques are handed down from bartender to bartender directly (or via internet posts these days) and become tribal knowledge. The methods shown in this book are the result of what I learned from various bartenders over the years, as well as through research and my own experiments. The names of each garnish are often not well defined. I have given names to each garnish in this book for the purpose of labeling, but they may be known to some people under a different moniker. Do not let the naming hold you back. Just focus on the techniques.

QUALITY OF INGREDIENTS

Most garnishes are based on fruit or other fresh produce. Though it sounds obvious, it's important to point out that you should always choose the best and freshest produce you can find for your garnishes. They are meant to add visual attractiveness to the cocktail and choosing dried-up, sad-looking fruit will have a negative effect on the appeal of the drink. Below are some tips for choosing quality ingredients.

As much as possible, select organic fruit, especially when the skin of the fruit is going to be exposed directly to the drink, as with a lemon twist or a floating citrus slice. You certainly don't want pesticides (and other toxic products sprayed on the fruit) to end up in your drink.

Choose citrus that have a colorful, shinny skin (more oil in it) and that feel firm to the touch.

Even with organic produce, you should still wash them thoroughly (you don't know how they were handled and what dirty paws have been groping them at the supermarket). If it is waxed, you can remove the wax by quick-boiling and scrubbing the fruit with a vegetable brush. And don't forget to remove the stickers. It sounds obvious, but you'd be surprised how many people forget this step, and I have seen it a number of times, even in professional bars.

All produce need to be fresh. So I recommend cutting the garnish on an as-needed basis. In a busy bar, I understand this is not always possible, so advance preparation is acceptable as long as you keep the garnishes cool and protected from oxidation (e.g. hold apple slices in acidulated water). Prepared garnishes can be kept in a fruit tray on ice. Make sure you keep the tray out of reach of guests, otherwise some people will just reach in (with potentially dirty hands) and grab a piece themselves (particularly olives and cherries).

Finally, it goes without saying that your hands should be absolutely clean when preparing garnishes. And even if you know your hands are clean, I recommend using mini-tongs to place fruit in the drink. It looks more professional and will make your germophobe guests feel more comfortable.

TOOLS

We all know the saying "a workman is only as good as his tools" and it's true for garnishes as well. Thankfully, the tool requirements for creating cocktail garnishes are pretty minimal. Below is a list of tools you are likely to need as well as some pointers on selecting quality ones and how to use them properly.

Cutting Board

You need a sturdy surface to cut fruit on, so a cutting board is essential. The most common materials are wood, rubber, and plastic. Keep the board clean and make sure you don't use the same board you used to cut meat. Also, make sure your cutting board is stable and will not slide. Place a damp towel underneath it if necessary.

Knives

Most garnishes require cutting fruits, and some require very accurate cuts. So it's important to have good knives. You will probably need two sizes:

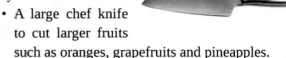

- A large chef knife to cut larger fruits such as oranges, grapefruits and pineapples.
- A smaller paring knife to cut the skin off and carve various shapes in the fruit or peel. Look for a length of 2.5" to 4".

In both cases, it's important that the blade be very sharp. It may be counter-intuitive, but a sharper knife is safer than a dull one, since it will slice cleanly (and with less pressure) and go where you want it to, whereas the dull one may slip and cause an accident. A lot of people swear by ceramic knives. They are indeed very sharp, but you need to handle them carefully, otherwise they will chip or break. Another popular option is the stainless steel blade with a non-stick coating. Both ceramic and coated knives come in a variety of colors, perfect if you want to express your garish side...

For precise cuts, I have seen people use an *xActo* knife. This works well, as they are very sharp and accurate. However, if you choose to use one, make sure it is clean and reserved only for this purpose (don't use the knife you used to cut carpet or vinyl tiles in your last redecoration project...)

Peeler

Peelers come in handy when slicing off a swath of citrus skin for a twist (see chapter 1), or slicing thin strips of cucumber for a ribbon (see chapter 6). A standard (vertical) vegetable peeler will work for most jobs, especially cutting long items. But some bartender prefer to use a so-called Y-peeler, as they feel it works better on round fruit such as citrus, which is what most garnishes are based on.

Channel Knife/Zester

This tool is very useful for cutting twists and spirals from citrus fruits or scoring a citrus for a  scored wheel (see chapter 1). It looks similar to a paring knife with a plastic handle, but the metal tip has a sharp V-shaped edge that protrudes downwards. By running this blade on a citrus skin, you can produce very clean strips. It usually also comes with a zester part which allows to extract zest from citrus. We also use it to score the peel of citrus.

Grater/Microplane

A grater can be used when grating spices or citrus zest on top of a cocktail. It can also  be used to grate ingredients for rims (see chapter 7). A microplane is a safer option because of its handle and, given its sharpness, it requires less effort.

Melon Baller

This one is pretty obvious. You will only need it when  making melon balls as explained in chapter 4.

Cocktail Sticks

A number of garnishes will be skewered on a stick. They can be as simple as a toothpick or a bit of skewer, but garnishes look much better with an attractive stick. They are available in bamboo or metal with pretty patterns on the end.

 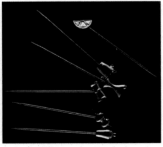

Offset Spatula

The offset spatula is used in pastry to spread creams, mousses or thick sauces. It is not used much in the cocktail world, but we use it for making chocolate garnishes (see chapter 10).

Mini-Torch

This small torch is typically used to caramelize the top of crème brûlées. In this book, we use it for a few garnishes such as caramelized bananas and cocktail *brûlé* (chapter 9).  It can also be used for flamed drinks in lieu of a match or lighter.

CHOOSING A GARNISH

While you have artistic license to decorate your cocktails as you see fit, there are some guidelines which will help you pick the best garnish for a given drink.

Below are some tips based on widely accepted industry standards. But feel free to experiment and get creative.

- Use a garnish that complements the main flavor in the drink (trying to match a minor flavor is less likely to succeed).
- If fresh citrus juice is featured in the drink, it makes sense to use the same citrus as a garnish.
- Citrus garnishes are not recommended for cream or dairy-based drinks.
- Fruity rum-based drinks are usually garnished with fresh tropical fruits.
- Tequila-based drinks usually pair well with lime garnishes.
- Gin-based drinks (such as Martinis) are generally paired with olives, onions or citrus twists.
- Tomato-based cocktails are usually garnished with limes, lemons and celery stalks.

The table on the following page lists the typical garnish for the most common cocktails.

TYPICAL GARNISHES

Cocktail	Garnish	Cocktail	Garnish
Alexander	Nutmeg sprinkle	Margarita	Salt rim and lime wedge
Americano	Lemon peel	Martini	Lemon twist or olive
Aviation	Cherry	Mint Julep	Mint sprig
Bloody Mary	Celery stalk & lemon wedge	Mojito	Mint sprig
Bramble	Blackberry and lemon slice	Moscow Mule	Lime wedge
Caipirinha	Sugar cane and lime	Negroni	Orange peel
Cape Cod	Lime wedge	Old Fashioned	Orange slice and cherry
Casino	Lemon twist and cherry	Pina Colada	Cherry/pineapple flag
Champagne Cocktail	Orange slice and cherry	Pisco Sour	Angostura bitters
Cosmopolitan	Lime wheel or wedge	Planter's Punch	Cherry/pineapple flag
Cuba Libre	Lime wedge	Porto Flip	Nutmeg sprinkle
Daiquiri	Lime half-wheel	Ramoz Gin Fizz	Orange half-wheel or peel
Dark & Stormy	Lime wedge	Rob Roy	Cherry or lemon twist
French 75	Lemon twist	Rose	Cherry
Gibson	Cocktail onion	Rusty nail	Lemon twist
Gimlet	Lime wedge or wheel	Sazerac	Lemon peel
Gin and Tonic	Lime wedge	Screwdriver	Orange slice
Grasshopper	Mint sprig	Sea Breeze	Lime wedge
Harvey Wallbanger	Orange slice and cherry	Sex on the Beach	Orange wheel
Horse's Neck	Lemon peel spiral	Sidecar	Sugar rim
Jack Rose	Cherry and apple slice	Singapore Sling	Cherry/pineapple flag
John Collins	Lemon slice and cherry	Tequila Sunrise	Cherry/orange flag
Long Island Iced Tea	Lemon wheel	Tom Collins	Cherry/orange flag
Mai Tai	Pineapple spear, mint leaves and lime peel	Vesper	Lemon peel
Manhattan	Cherry	Whiskey Sour	Orange half-wheel and cherry

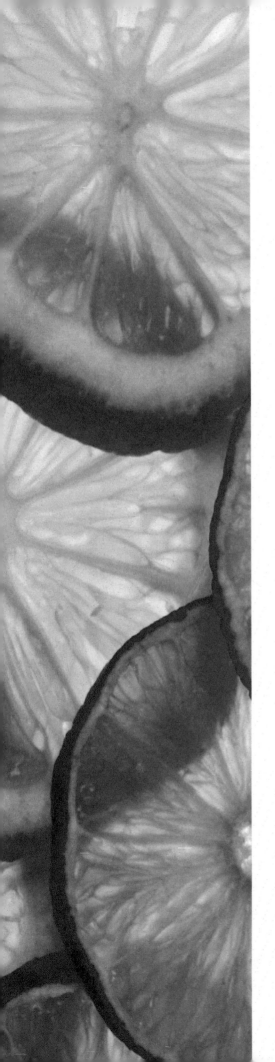

Chapter 1 – Citrus

Citrus fruits are the most common cocktail garnish. They are relatively cheap, can be cut in a variety of simple shapes, and their peel contains oils that contribute to the flavor of the drink. Also, since citrus are part of a number of cocktails in the form of a juice, they make a natural garnish partner for those drinks.

In this section, we discuss the most common citrus types: lemons, limes and oranges and how they are used as garnish. We go over detailed instructions to make simple citrus garnishes including wedges, wheels, strips, swaths and spirals.

We then build upon these simple structures and create interesting variations on the classics.

Finally, we cover some more sophisticated citrus garnishes which require a bit more patience and practice, but are well worth the effort.

INTRODUCTION

This section briefly describes the parts of a citrus fruit and discusses the three main citrus types and their use as cocktail garnishes.

Since the cuts are very similar for the different varieties, the step-by-step instructions in this chapter will be given generically, instead of repeating the information for each type. Different citrus varieties will be used to illustrate each cut, but you can substitute as you wish. You will need to keep size in mind, however. Some oranges and grapefruits are pretty big, and depending on the size on the glassware, the garnish could be overwhelming. Use common sense and adjust the cuts as needed.

Anatomy of a Citrus Fruit

During the course of this chapter, I will refer to the various parts of citrus fruits. For those who are not familiar with those terms, this section provides a quick guide to those parts.

- *Peel/skin/zest*: the outside part of the fruit (yellow, orange or green depending on the type). This is the part that contains the citrus oils.
- *Flesh/pulp*: the inside of the fruit that is juicy and comes in segments.
- *Pith*: the white layer that sits between the flesh and the skin. It is usually bitter.
- *Stem*: the end of the fruit where it was hanging from the tree.
- *Stylar*: the opposite end of the fruit

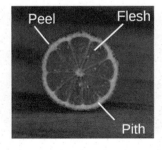

Limes

Native of South Asia (like most citrus), limes are now widely used around the world. Their juice was used by the British Navy to prevent scurvy, and now they are a staple of any bar. They are the most acidic of the common citrus (pH 1.8-2.4) and contain little sugar, so they bring a more bitter and astringent taste to drinks than lemons, but the complexities of the lime flavors do provide for a more interesting cocktail.

In general, limes tend to work better with drinks based on gin, blanco tequila and light rum. They are the typical garnish for classic cocktails such as the Gin & Tonic, the Cape Cod, the Seabreeze, the Margarita and the Cuba Libre. They can also be used in Bloody Marys and muddled into Mojitos and Caipirinhas. Finally, any lime-based cocktail can usually benefit from a lime garnish.

Lemons

Lemons have a long culinary history as well. But for a long time, they were expensive, and only the wealthy could afford them. They are slightly less acidic (pH 2-2.5) and a little sweeter than limes.

Lemons tend to pair well with barrel-aged liquors such as whiskey, reposado and añejo tequilas, brandies and dark rums. As a result, they will also be a good garnish for cocktails based on these spirits. They also work well with iced teas, cola-based drinks and lemonades.

The peel/twist is the most common way to use it (as in the Americano, the Martini, the Sazerac or the Rusty Nail), but sometimes a wheel is used (for instance in a Long Island Iced Tea or a Bramble).

Oranges

Oranges are the least acidic of the three (pH 3-4.5) and are a lot sweeter (which results a richer mouth feel). Their use in cocktails is a little less common than limes and lemons. When you use them, keep in mind the sweetness they are adding, otherwise you may end up with too sweet a drink.

In terms of garnish, since most oranges are bigger than limes and lemons, they may look out of place on a small glass. A common way oranges are used as a garnish is with a cherry, in the form of a flag or a boat (see chapter 5).

WEDGES

The citrus wedge is the most common cocktail garnish. It serves a dual function: it decorates the glass and offers the drinker the ability to increase the sourness of the drink by squeezing more juice into it.

That is, of course, as long as the bartender leaves the wedge on the glass. There is considerable debate as to whether the bartender should squeeze the citrus in for the guest or not. Some argue that squeezing the wedge can be a messy job, and that we should help the guest not get their hands sticky. They may have a point, but we also have to keep in mind that people have different tastes. Some prefer their drinks on the sweet side, some more on the sour side. Unless you know the guest's preference or they have asked specifically, it's best to give them the option to add sourness after they tasted the drink. This is similar to offering salt and pepper for a dish. Another reason for not dropping the wedge in the glass is that it can be seen as unsanitary. The more germophobe among us may not trust the bartender's hands to be perfectly clean (after all they are handling dirty glasses, towels, money, ...) and would get repulsed by the idea of a manually-handled piece of fruit being dropped in their drink.

If you leave the option for the guest to squeeze the wedge, give them an extra napkin so they can wipe their hands if juice were to drip on them. If the guest does request that you squeeze the wedge, then make sure to cup your hand on the other side to protect him/her from accidental squirts.

If you're going to serve a wedge of citrus as a garnish, make sure it is big and juicy, giving the drinker not only a nice-looking garnish but also the option to squeeze more juice. It is very disappointing to be served a drink with a razor-thin wedge or half a wedge. It may save the bar a few pennies, but this is a short-sighted saving in my opinion, as it lowers the quality of the final product.

The attention to quality starts at the market. Choose citrus fruits that have a nice colorful and thin skin (relatively firm to the touch) but also feel heavy for their size (a sign that they are juicy).

Another source of debate is whether to trim the ends (stem and stylar) before cutting into wedges. Some argue that leaving them on gives the fruit a more natural shape and is less likely to be messy when squeezed. Others prefer the neater appearance of the cut fruit. There's no right or wrong answer; it's a matter of personal choice. My preference is to trim the ends, following the natural shape of the fruit (skip step one if you disagree).

1. Trim the stem and stylar, rounding the ends, keeping the natural curve of the fruit.
2. Slice the fruit completely in half lengthwise.
3. On both halves of the fruit, cut a perpendicular slit halfway through the flesh (but not the skin). This will be the slit on each wedge that allows you to attach the fruit to the rim, and it's easier to cut them at this stage rather than through each wedge individually. The exception is if you want unusual angles (see section below on angled wedges).
4. Lay the piece flat.
5. Depending on the size of the fruit, cut each piece
   a) In half and in half again (yielding a total of four wedges from each half).
   or
   b) In thirds (yielding three wedges from each half).
6. Remove the seeds.
7. Place on the glass using the slit.

Variation

Instead of making a slit through the flesh of the wedge to hang it on the rim, you can cut the peel half way up and slide it on the glass between peel and flesh.

Angled Wedge

You don't have to limit yourself to vertical or horizontal angles. Feel free to adjust the cuts to any angle. You can also cut the wedge through the skin instead of the flesh, but be careful not to cut too deep into the flesh or the piece will break.

1. Start with a lemon wedge
2. Cut a notch through the skin at a 45 degree angle, a third of the way from the end. Don't go too deep.
3. Hang on top of the glass.

Scored Wedge

To give your wedge a more interesting look, you can score the skin with a zester before cutting into wedges. You can draw any pattern you like, but it looks more impressive if you have lines in different directions. The most basic scoring is a criss-cross:

1. Use a zester and score a lime from top to bottom but at an angle.
2. Score in the opposite direction creating an X pattern
3. Repeat steps 1 and 2 until the entire lime is scored in a criss-cross pattern.
4. Cut into wedges as normal

Here's a more interesting example that has some scoring in two perpendicular directions as well as a bit of unscored peel.

1. Use a zester and score a lime around the equator.
2. Score the lime from above the scored lines of the equator to the top of the lime on four sides.
3. Score the lime from below the scored lines of the equator to the bottom of the lime on four sides. But score where there was no scoring on the top part so the scoring is not aligned.
4. Cut the lime in half from stem to stylar following the edge of a score.
5. Cut into the flesh (this will be the notch to hang on the glass).
6. Cut each half into four wedges following the score limits.

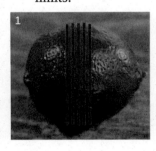

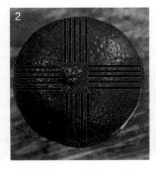

Wedge with Partially Cut-off Peel

This technique does not produce a finished garnish, but it is the first step of the next few garnishes. So, instead of repeating these steps over and over, I will describe them here once and refer to them in the subsequent sections. In these sections, I will illustrate the technique with a lemon, but feel free to use any citrus for any of these garnishes (keeping in mind of course the size of your glassware).

1. Cut a citrus wedge.
2. Place the wedge skin down on a board.
3. Using a sharp paring knife, slice through the pith, cutting the peel off about three quarters of the way.
4. Slice off some pith from the skin to make it more pliable (see tips on page 23)
5. You end up with a wedge that has three quarters of its peel dangling

Sliver "Tuck-under"

This variation on a standard citrus wedge is fairly easy, but it adds quite a bit of flair to the garnish. It involves slicing part of the peel off, then tucking a sliver of that skin under to create a loop.

1. Follow the steps for the "Wedge with partially cut-off peel".
2. Cut a sliver on the side of the skin (do not cut all the way through).
3. Tuck the skin on itself with the sliver sticking out.
4. Cut a diagonal notch in the flesh of the fruit (to hang on rim).
5. Place on rim of glass.

Double Sliver "Tuck-under"

Here's another variation on the same theme as the previous two techniques. This time, we are cutting slivers on both sides of the skin, creating a V-shaped sliver that sticks out. The wedge is also hung in a different way: instead of cutting a notch in the flesh, we hang the garnish with the glass between the flesh and skin (slivers pointing down).

1. Follow the steps for the "Wedge with partially cut-off peel".
2. Cut a sliver on each side of the skin (be careful not to cut all the way through).
3. Tuck the center of the skin under.
4. Slide on the rim, flesh hanging inside the glass.

Citrus Pinwheel

This technique is similar to the previous one, but this time we are cutting a series on slivers in the skin. When the skin is tucked under, the slivers fan out creating a pinwheel effect.

1. Follow the steps for the "Wedge with partially cut-off peel".
2. Cut diagonal notches on one side of the skin (be careful to not slice all the way across).
3. Tuck the end of the skin under.
4. This will fan out the slivers cut in the previous step.
5. Cut a diagonal notch in the flesh and hang on the rim.

V-Neck

The cut for this technique is similar to the previous one, but this time we actually cut out a V-shaped piece of peel instead of leaving it attached to the main piece. The garnish is hung on the rim using a standard notch, and we slide in the cut-out V upside down between the skin and the flesh.

1. Follow the steps for the "Wedge with partially cut-off peel".
2. Cut a V off the end of the skin.

13

3. Cut a diagonal notch in the flesh and hang on the rim.
4. Slide the cut-out V between the skin and the flesh, points facing up.
5. Slightly curl the ends of the V outward.

Peel Horns

Here's another example in our series of tucked-under peels. In this case, we cut a W shape out of the middle of the peel. This results in two horns sticking away from the wedge.

1. Follow the steps for the "Wedge with partially cut-off peel".
2. Cut a slit on each side of the skin.
3. Cut a V in the middle (do not cut through to the outside). You will end up with a W-shaped cut.
4. Push the center out; be careful to not break it off.
5. Tuck the end of the skin under. You will end up with 2 triangles of skin pointing outwards looking somewhat like horns.
6. Cut a notch in the flesh and hang on the rim.

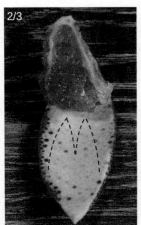

Double-Point

Here's a final variation on this theme. This time, two Vs are cut in the peel (one inside the other). When tucked under, two points will stick outwards at different angles.

1. Follow the steps for the "Wedge with partially cut-off peel".
2. Cut 2 elongated and slightly curved Vs (one inside the other) in the middle of the skin.
3. Pull the 2 Vs through and pull the center V through further.
4. Tuck the center of the skin under. You will end up with 2 triangles pointing out at different angles.
5. Cut a diagonal notch in the flesh.
6. Hang on rim.

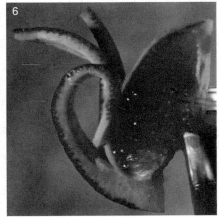

Wheels

The citrus wheel (also called slice) is a ubiquitous garnish that can be positioned on the rim of the glass or dropped in the drink for added flavor. They are typically used for Screwdrivers, Pimm's Cups and Gin Fizzes.

1. Cut the ends of the citrus.
2. Cut the citrus crosswise in ¼" slices.
3. Lay the wheels flat on the cutting board.
4. Cut a slit from the middle of each wheel to its edge.
5. Place vertically on the rim using the slit.

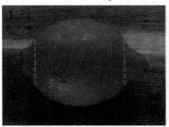

Note that you can cut a smaller slit (only through the skin and not the flesh) if you want the wheel to sit higher on the glass. But keep in mind that this is less stable.

Half and Quarter Wheels

You can cut the wheel in half (or even in quarters for large oranges). You can attach the half or quarter wheel to the rim using a simple slit but now you have the option to orient the garnish at any angle.

The most obvious position is horizontal but you can also align it vertically or at an angle as described below.

Vertical Half-Wheel

1. Start with a lemon half-wheel.
2. Cut a slit parallel to the inner edge going about one third of the way into the flesh.
3. Hang on rim.

Angled Half-Wheel

You can tweak the previous technique by adjusting the position of the slit depending on the orientation of the garnish that you want.

Citrus Moon

You can create a whimsical variation of the angled half-wheel by cutting out part of the flesh to create a crescent shape.

1. Start with a half-wheel.
2. Using a sharp knife, cut out an oblong sliver (crescent) at the edge of the flesh. You can also use a cookie cutter, but make sure it is sharp enough to cut the flesh and not crush it.
3. Cut a slit in the skin about three quarters of the way down the edge (do not go too deep into the flesh or it will break apart when lifted).
4. Hang on glass facing outwards using the slit.

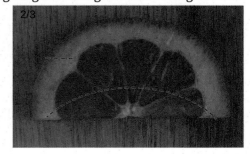

Offset Half-Wheel

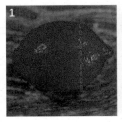

You can create an interesting dropped garnish by pinning two half-wheels together and offseting them.

1. Start with citrus wheel.
2. Cut the wheel in half.
3. Place the half-wheels on top each other with a slight offset.
4. Secure with a cocktail stick in the center and near the skin.
5. Drop in the drink.

Dropped Wheel

You can drop a wheel in the drink and float it on top instead of hanging it on the rim.

In this case, the wheel is usually cut thinner.

Note that this will add more citrus flavor to the drink. So keep that in mind as you balance the drink.

Twisted Wheel

Here's a simple dropped garnish based on a citrus wheel.

1. Start with a citrus wheel.
2. Slice the wheel from the center to the edge.
3. Twist the sides in opposite directions.
4. Place on the glass or drop in the drink.

Notched Wheel

For a more interesting look, before cutting it, score the citrus using a channel knife. This will give your wheels indentations.

1. Hold the citrus firmly in one hand and a channel knife in the other.
2. Cut notches over the entire fruit, from stem to stylar, straight or diagonally.
3. Slice the fruit as described earlier and cut a slit from center to edge.
4. Hang on the rim or float on the drink.

Double Twist

This is a pretty cool dropped garnish made by twisting 2 slices of citrus.

1. Cut the end of the fruit.
2. Start cutting a thin slice but only go half way.
3. Cut a slice (fully this time) next to the previous cut. You will have two thin slices attached partially.
4. Cut a slit from the center to the edge of the attached side.
5. Hold the fruit on both sides of the slit, twist and separate the sides.
6. Drop in drink.

16

Half-Wheel "Tuck-under"

A nice variation on a half-wheel involves cutting the skin off partially and tucking it under to form a loop.

1. Start with a ¼" half-wheel.
2. Using a sharp paring knife, cut through the pith about ¾ of the way. The skin should now be mostly separated from the flesh with ¼ remaining attached.
3. Tuck the skin under to form a loop.
4. Cut a small slit in the flesh.
5. Hang on rim using the slit.

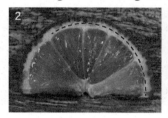

Ring Wheel

This garnish involves cutting the skin almost all around a citrus wheel and hanging on the glass between the skin and the flesh.

1. Start with a citrus wheel.
2. With a sharp knife, pierce the pith.
3. Cut through the pith almost all the way around (stop before you reach the starting point, leaving ½-1" still attached).
4. Push the flesh through the peel (be careful not break the connection).
5. Hang over the rim (ring on the outside and flesh on the inside).
6. Place straw through the ring.

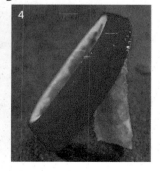

Wheel With Peel "Roll Around"

This is a simple variation on a wheel where the skin is peeled off partially and rolled in a loop.

1. Cut a ½" wheel out of a citrus.
2. Cut the skin off almost all the way around; stop before you reach the starting point, so that the skin remains attached.
3. Continue the cut to the edge of the skin.
4. Roll the dangling skin on itself so that it curves more.
5. Cut a slit from center to edge and slide on the glass.

Wheel With Peel "Loop-Through"

Here's another interesting variation on a wheel, where the peel is cut around the outside and looped through the middle. This technique is a little more tricky as you need to cut half the width of the peel. So use a sharp knife, and be careful as you cut so that the strips are of an even width.

1. Cut out a ½" citrus wheel.
2. Start slicing half the width of the skin off.
3. Continue slicing half the skin width until you almost reach the starting point, but stop before you get there (the skin should remain attached). Ensure the strip is as even as possible.
4. Turn the wheel around.
5. Starting at the same point you stopped slicing the first half skin, start slicing the other half of the skin in the opposite direction.

6. Continue slicing this half-width skin until you almost reach the starting point, but stop before you get there (the skin should remain attached). You should now have two dangling bits of skins.

7. Poke a hole in the center of the wheel with a skewer.

8. Push one piece of dangling skin into the hole on one side and the other piece on the other side (let the skin come out the other side a little).

9. Pull on the bits poking through to tighten the loops a little.

10. Cut a slit at the bottom of the wheel.

11. Slide the slit on the rim.

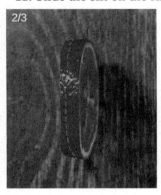

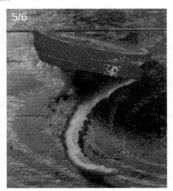

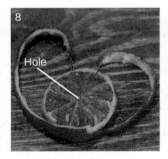

Citrus Stack

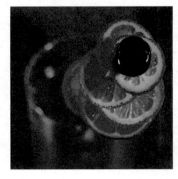

This is an architectural garnish that adds height to the drink. It is built by stacking thin slices of citrus (both lime and lemon) on a skewer at a slight offset. To hide the tip of the skewer and provide a nice contrast, it is best to top it off with a berry or cherry.

1. Cut 4 thin slices from the end of a lime (discard the very tip).

2. Cut 4 thin slices from the end of a lemon (discard the very tip).

3. Thread a cherry on a skewer.

4. For each slice in increasing order of size.

   a) Cut a slit from the center to the edge.

   b) Overlap the two sides of the slit to create a slight curve in the slice.

   c) Thread on the skewer, making sure the skewer goes through the overlapped sides to keep them in place.

   d) Push the slice all the way to the top.

   e) Do not line up the slices. Instead alternate the offset to create an uneven distribution.

5. Place skewer in the drink

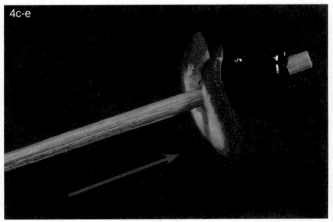

SPIRALS

This section is dedicated to spiral-shaped citrus garnishes. As usual, we build up from the simple twist to more tricky techniques (such as the horse's neck or the orange rose).

Twist

The citrus twist is an elegant spiral-like garnish that hangs on top of the glass or is dropped in the drink. It is a typical garnish for highball drinks and martinis among others. Creating a twist involves removing a thin strip of peel and curling it on itself to create a spiral. There are a couple of methods to do this.

Method 1

1. Hold the fruit firmly in one hand and a channel knife in the other. It is recommended to hold it over the drink, so that the oils squirt into it as you cut.
2. Cut out a strip around the fruit (horizontally, not top to bottom). It's easier if you turn the fruit instead of the knife. You can make the strip as long as you like. This takes a little practice so be patient and don't worry if your first attempt is not great.
3. Twist the peel around a cocktail stick, skewer or straw and hold for a bit. The peel will hold its shape.
4. Hang on rim or drop in drink.

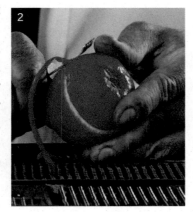

Method 2

1. Cut a citrus wheel (see previous section).
2. Lay the wheel flat on a cutting board.
3. Using a paring knife vertically, cut between the pith and the flesh of the fruit all the way around.
4. Separate the flesh from the skin.
5. Cut the skin at one point on the circle.
6. Twist the peel around a cocktail stick, skewer or straw and hold for a bit as described earlier.
7. Hang on rim or drop in drink.

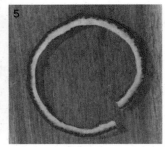

Variation

Usually the spiral is kept fairly short, but why not create a longer one spanning the rim (method 1 needs to be used in this case).

Citrus Swirl

This garnish is less common than the twist but is also an attractive option. It is more two-dimensional and resembles a flat spiral rather than a coil.

1. Cut the ends of the fruit.
2. Make a cut in the skin (not the flesh) along the length.
3. Peel the skin off the flesh.
4. Roll the skin tightly (like a jelly roll) and secure with toothpicks.
5. Place the roll in a bowl of water and refrigerate for 2 hours.
6. Slice strips of the desired width.
7. Hang on rim of the glass or drop in drink.

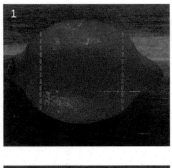

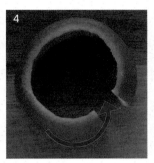

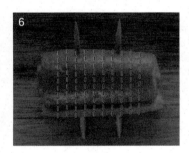

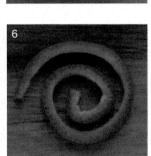

7. When you get to the end, place the round circle on top the wrapped peel. This will actually be the bottom of the finished product.
8. Flip the "flower" over.
9. Place a small skewer through the rose to hold things together and hang on glass.
10. Optionally add a sprig of mint to the side of the flower.

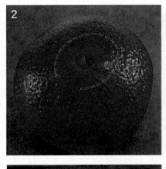

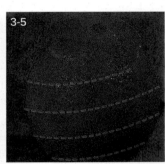

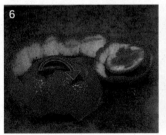

Orange Rose

The orange rose is a very elegant garnish created by rolling a full orange spiral on itself to create the illusion of a rose. A sprig of mint is usually added for contrast.

1. Select an orange that is fairly round and has good-looking skin.
2. Using a paring knife, start at the bottom of the orange, and cut a circle as a starting point. Obviously, do not cut all the way through, otherwise you will not be able to continue the strip.
3. Start cutting around the orange, making a ½"strip.
4. Continue going all the way around the orange, trying to keep the strip width even. Take your time, be careful and make sure you do not break the peel.
5. When you get near the top, let the strip get thin until it ends in a point.
6. Starting from the end point (the thin pointy side you ended with), start wrapping the peel on itself tightly.

Variations
- You can use the same technique with lemon, apple or pear peels.
- For a simpler but also less bulky version, you can use a smaller piece of peel, roll it around a dowel, and cut a slit at the bottom to hang on the glass.

Horse's Neck

The Horse's neck is another classic spiral peel garnish; it consists of a long strip of lemon peel wrapped on the inside of the glass. It is typically used for the drink of the same name (a mix of brandy or bourbon and ginger ale), but nothing prevents you from using it on other drinks.

1. Using a paring knife, start at the bottom of the lemon and cut a circle as a starting point. Do not cut all the way through, otherwise you will not be able to continue the strip.
2. Carefully continue cutting a ¼" to ½" strip all around the lemon to make a spiral. Don't worry if you have a little white pith on the back. It will actually make the spiral sturdier in the glass.
3. Place the piece on a cutting board and even out the edges.
4. Coil the peel around your finger or bar spoon (or simply twist the piece on itself).
5. Place spiral inside a Collins or highball glass, leaving one end hanging over the rim of the glass. You may want to cut a small slit in the peel to help it hang on the glass.
6. Using a bar spoon to hold the spiral in place, pour the drink in the glass.

Variations
- Use a channel knife to make a much thinner strip and roll inside the glass as described above.
- You can make the garnish with an orange peel as well, and use it in a variety of drinks, in particular tiki-style drinks.

Pinwheel

This garnish is another elegant way to decorate a drink. It involves wrapping a fringed spiral of orange peel on itself and results in a garnish that gives the impression of a pinwheel.

1. Cut a small spiral out of an orange (see previous page). You only need a quarter of the orange peel.
2. Straighten the edges by slicing off ragged bits.
3. With the pith facing up, cut parallel diagonal lines on the outside of the spiral.
4. Starting at the top, roll the spiral peel very tightly and secure with a toothpick (break off excess toothpick).
5. Place on top of drink.

Wheel with a Twist

For an interesting combination of wheel and twist techniques, you can:

1. Partially cut the peel off of a citrus wheel.

2. Twist the peel around a cocktail stick or straw as described earlier.

This results in a very elegant wheel with a dangling twist.

Variation

You can create a similar garnish with just a half-wheel instead of a full wheel. Cut the garnish as described above and cut away the half of the flesh that does not have the peel attached.

Tying the Knot

The knot is a simple but elegant way to finish a cocktail. Though not technically a spiral, this garnish fits in this category of citrus strips twisted into shape. It is basically a strip tied into a loop and dropped in the drink.

1. Create a citrus strip using one of the methods described earlier in this chapter.
2. Loop one end of the strip.
3. Thread the other end through it, creating a knot.
4. Drop in drink.

PEEL/SWATH

The citrus peel (sometimes also called swath) is a very simple garnish, which (if done right) also impart delicate citrus flavors to the drink through the expression of the oils in the skin. The oils provide an aroma that gives another dimension to the drink. This is called a "twist" by some, but for others a "twist" is a spiral-like strip described in the previous section. Regardless of what you call it, this is a quintessential garnish for Martinis, Boulevardiers, Negronis and other elegant drinks.

Since the oil content of the skin is crucial, make sure you choose fruits that have a shiny skin and feel ripe (but not mushy). An old dried skin will not have much oil and will look lame in your drink.

Basic Method

1. Hold the fruit in one hand and, using a peeler or paring knife, cut a wide swath of skin from one end to the other. Use one smooth motion instead of starts and stops. Also take care to not include too much pith (looking at it from the back you should be able to see the pores). If you have a lot of pith on the skin, lay it on a board and slice it off (see tips on the next page).

2. Express the oils on the surface of the drink. A couple of options:

   a) Hold the peel a few inches over the drink between thumb and index fingers, the peel side facing the drink, then squeeze the sides of the peel.

   b) Hold the two sides of the peel between thumb and index fingers of both hands (peel side facing the drink) and twist.

3. Wipe the peel all around the outside of the glass (hold the stem of the glass with the other hand to stabilize it).

4. Drop the peel in the drink. As with the wedge, this step is optional and subject to debate among bartenders.

Peel-off Method

An efficient way to prepare a number of peels ahead of time is to use the "peel off" method. Using this technique, your swaths are pre-cut and ready to be peeled off, while remaining fresh. This is especially practical in a busy bar.

1. Make incisions through the skin and pith (but not the flesh) of the fruit from stylar to stem all the way around the fruit. The spacing of the cut is up to you depending how wide you want your swaths to be.
2. Cut one end of the fruit.
3. When you need a swath, just peel it off the fruit.
4. Proceed with the expression of the oils and presentation as above.

 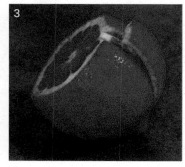

Tips for Cutting Pith off Skin

When using a piece of citrus skin, it is best to remove most of the white pith to avoid adding bitterness to the drink. If your initial cut included too much pith, you can remove it by following these guidelines:

- Make sure the skin is at room temperature (it will be less brittle).
- Lay the skin flat on a board, pith-side up.
- Hold a paring knife flat, and carefully slice off a layer of pith.
- Work on the edge of your work surface, so that your hand can be level with the skin.
- Keep your knife very flat (watch both sides of the knife so that it does not dip down, otherwise it will cut into the skin).

- Do several passes if necessary. It is better to remove a few thin slices than try to do it all at once and accidentally cut through the skin.
- When done, you should have a thin strip of peel with little pith as shown here. The pores should be visible.

Scored Swath

To jazz up a swath, you can score the fruit first before peeling it. Drag a zester across the skin to score it. You can draw any design you like, but it looks better if you have lines going in different direction. See for example the scoring we used on a wedge on page 12.

Shaped Swath

Some bartenders like to even out the sides of the swath to give it a more geometric shape. Common shapes are rectangles or triangles, but you can get creative and cut any shape you find attractive.

You can also use a cookie cutter to cut the desired shape from the peel. Or you can use a knife for a more intricate shapes. Here's an example of a martini glass.

Finally, how about shaping two swaths into a heart:

1. Cut the peel off a ½" wide citrus wheel.
2. Cut the peel in half.
3. Fold the two sides to form a heart.
4. Secure with a toothpick at the bottom.

Slotted Swath

In this garnish, we jazz up a swath by slicing lines in the middle and curling it a little. Note that, due to its fragility, it's not really possible to express the oils once it is cut. So it is mostly visual. If you want the oil flavors, express them from normal swath first before adding this garnish.

1. Cut a large swath from a citrus.
2. Cut the swath into a parallelogram.
3. Using a sharp knife, make incisions in the middle of the piece, parallel to the long side, about 2-3mm apart.
4. Wrap the piece around a chopstick and let it sit for 2-3 minutes.
5. Remove from the chopstick and gently separate the curls.
6. Drop in the drink

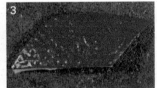

Citrus Wings

Here is a simple but elegant garnish that looks like wings of citrus hanging on the rim of the glass. It is created by creasing a swath and cutting a slit in the middle.

1. Cut a small citrus swath into an oblong shape.
2. Cut a lengthwise slit in the middle of the swath.
3. Curve or crease the swath.
4. Place on rim using the slit.

A CUT ABOVE

This section contains techniques that are a little more advanced. If you are new to garnishes, you may want to start with the simpler garnishes shown earlier. If you have been using the techniques in the previous sections, then you should be able to pick these up, as they build upon them. Some of you may consider the garnishes over-the-top. They are certainly a lot bigger and more "in your face", but for the right cocktail, they are a beautiful addition.

Lemon Slivered Loop

This garnish is built from a lemon wheel. It results in a loop of peel hanging off the wheel, with beautiful slivers fanning out around it.

1. Cut a ¾" wide wheel off the center of a large lemon.
2. Cut the skin off almost all the way around. Stop before you reach the starting point; the skin should remain attached.
3. Lay the piece on a board with the pith side up.
4. Slice some of the pith off the skin (see tips on page 23).
5. Slice thin slivers off the right side of the skin.
6. Roll the skin back on itself to form a loop and secure with a toothpick.
7. Place the wheel on top of the glass at the desired angle and mark the angle of the slit following the side of the glass.
8. Cut the marked slit and slide on glass.
9. Add a cherry to the end of the toothpick.

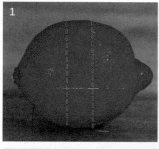

5. Cut a diagonal line across the parallel lines.
6. Loop the piece on itself. You end up with a loop on both sides and dangling strips between them.
7. Place a mint leaf in the middle and secure with a toothpick.
9. Place a cherry on the toothpick.
10. Set on drink.

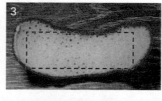
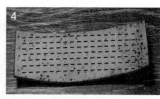

Lemon Burst

This is a very elegant garnish with numerous slivers bursting out of a center cherry. It requires precise cuts, so take your time, and do not be discouraged if it does not work the first time. It is best to start with a room temperature lemon so that the skin is easier to work with.

1. Cut a large swath out of a lemon.
2. Slice pith off. This will make the peel more pliable (see tips on page 23).
3. Cut the sides off to make straight edges.
4. Slice a number of parallel lines on the inside.

Orange Scarf

This is a very impressive garnish with slivers of peel wrapping lovingly around the glass like a scarf.
This garnish works best on a large highball glass (since it takes up a lot of space).

1. Cut a 1" wide slice out of an orange.
2. Slice off the skin.
3. Repeat steps 1 and 2 with another orange.
4. Lay peel flat on a board and remove the excess pith (see tips on page 23). You don't have to remove all of it, just make it level.
5. Stack the two rectangles and cut to make them the same size.

6. With the pith facing up, slice parallel diagonal lines on the right side of one of the rectangles.

7. With the orange side facing up, slice parallel diagonal lines on the right side of the other rectangle.

8. Place the pith side of the two rectangles together at the top, slivers facing down and overlapping in the middle. Secure with a toothpick.

9. Wrap the two sides of the rectangle around the glass and secure at the bottom with a small piece of toothpick.

10. Add a cherry on the top and bottom toothpick.

Lemon Sunshine

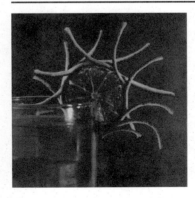

Here's another interesting decoration that gives the impression of sun rays bursting out of a lemon. It is made by cutting slivers into the skin in a similar manner to what we did in previous garnishes.

1. Cut a ¾" wide slice out of a large lemon (keeping the "flat" middle part and cutting when it rounds off).

2. Cut the skin off with as little pith as possible. Reserve the lemon flesh.

3. Remove any excess pith (see tips on page 23). This will make the skin more pliable.

4. Cut the ends off to even out the piece and make a rectangle.

5. Lay the rectangle flat (skin side down), and cut parallel diagonal lines along the right side, smaller at the top and longer at the bottom.

6. Turn the piece 180 degrees, and cut similar lines on the other side. Be careful that your cuts do not meet the cuts on the other side, otherwise your piece will not remain together.

7. Wrap the cut peel around the reserved lemon flesh, skin side facing in, and secure with a toothpick on each side

8. Cut a small slit at the bottom between the two toothpicks.

9. Place on the rim using the slit.

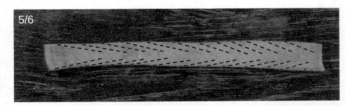

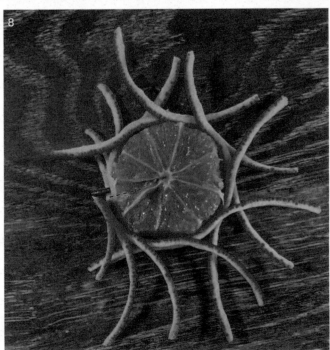

Orange Butterfly

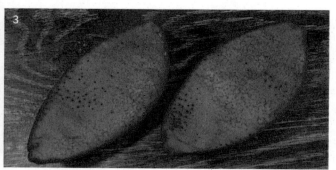

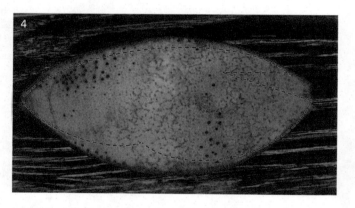

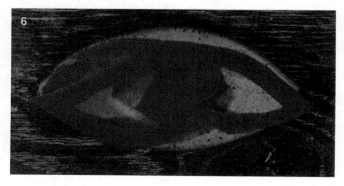

Here's a pretty whimsical garnish representing a butterfly on the edge of the glass.

Precise cuts are required. Use the pattern in the illustrations as a guide, but feel free to adapt the design to your taste. Your cuts don't have to be exactly like mine, as long as you make the two pieces symmetrical as explained in step 6.

1. Score the skin of an orange to delineate quarters (cut through the skin and pith but not into the flesh).
2. Slide your fingers under the skin and remove two skin "quarters".
3. Lay the skins flat, pith side up and slice off the pith (this will make the skin more pliable). See tips on page 23.
4. Lay one of the pieces flat, pith-side up, and cut based on the pattern shown in figure 4.
5. Flip the piece over and cut out inside shapes based on figure 5.
6. Place the two pieces on top of each other (pith sides together), and cut the second piece using the already cut piece as a template.
7. Hold the 2 pieces together to form the butterfly.
8. Place on top of the glass at the desired angle.
9. Place a knife along the top of the glass (following the direction of the glass), and cut up into the two skins to make slits.
10. Slide the slits onto the glass. If you cut along the direction of the glass the butterfly, will be positioned at the correct angle.

Chapter 2 – Cherries & Berries

This chapter covers two attractive red fruit categories: cherries and berries.

Cherries are widely used, but their quality is usually questionable. We will discuss how to buy and make quality cherries, as well as how to use them as garnishes.

Berries tend to be less commonly used than citrus and cherries, in large part due to their higher cost. But they can provide very attractive garnishes and add a welcome splash of color to the cocktail. We will cover garnishing techniques related to strawberries, lychees, blueberries and other berries. We also discuss the use of berries in a cocktail category called "cobblers".

CHERRIES

After citrus, the cherry is the most popular garnish, either on its own or as part of a flag or boat (see chapter 5). They have been used as a garnish since the 1800s for drinks like the Manhattan or the Bijou, and are the typical garnish for cocktails such as Manhattan, Amaretto Sour, Tom Collins, Whiskey Sour, Shirley Temple as well as tropical drinks and drinks topped with whipped cream.

Unfortunately, in most bars, the cherries are of very poor quality, which has given this garnish a bad rap. In this section, we will not only cover the most common ways to use cherries as a garnish, but also discuss how to buy quality cherries and also how to prepare your own.

The Infamous Maraschino Cherry

Maraschino cherries have not always been the hideous, super-processed, overly sweet, bright red abominations we know today. Originally, they were made from Croatian or Italian *Marasca* cherries, steeped in Maraschino liqueur, and they were delicious. But, they were also expensive, so around the turn of the 20th century, enterprising American producers started creating cheaper replicas with local supplies. This, combined with the demands of the temperance movement for non-alcoholic cherries, led to this sub-standard product becoming the norm... to this day.

Those cherries you find at the grocery store are a marvel of the food industry: first the cherries are soaked in a chemical brine, which firms them up but also robs them of their color. They are then rinsed and jarred with corn-syrup, artificial flavorings, chemical preservatives and FD&C Red #40. Sounds delicious, doesn't it?

But do not despair, the following section will show you how to acquire or prepare quality cherries.

Commercial Cherries

Thankfully, quality Maraschino cherries have not been fully eradicated from our stores. In particular, the Italian company *Luxardo* makes an excellent product, true to the original method. The texture has just the right

firmness in my opinion along with a complex flavor profile, which includes hints of spices, wood and vanilla. They can be found in good liquor stores and online, but they are quite pricey. *Fabbri* also makes good Amarena cherries in a nice decorative jar, but they are quite expensive too. A cheaper alternative is *Toschi Amarena*. These wild Italian cherries are preserved in syrup, and are not quite up to *Luxardo*'s standard, but they are pretty good, especially considering the price difference.

Some people discard the syrup that comes in the jar and replace it with brandy and other liqueurs they like. If you want to try this, let the cherries steep for a few weeks so they have time to absorb the flavors.

Note that the quality cherries such as *Luxardo*'s tend to be very dark in color (almost black). In the illustrations of this and subsequent chapters, I will use these cherries rather than the bright red ones you may be used to. This means that the garnishes using these cherries may look a little different to what most people expect. I hope more bartenders start using quality cherries, and over time redefine the expectation of what a standard cocktail cherry looks and tastes like.

Homemade Maraschino Cherries

Making your own Maraschino cherries is quite easy, and gives you lots of flexibility to match the flavor profile you prefer (see variations below the recipe). At a high level, the procedure involves simply steeping cherries in syrup and Maraschino liqueur. This liqueur is made from the small sour *Marasca* cherries (which grow in Croatia and part of Italy). *Luxardo* is the best and most well-known brand, and bottles of Maraschino liqueur can be purchased in good liquor stores.

If you want to be true to tradition, use *Marasca* cherries. These can be hard to find so you can also use local cherries (such as Morelos or Bings). Fresh cherries are best, but if necessary you can use canned or frozen cherries.

The following recipe makes about a quart.

Ingredients

- 1 pound of cherries (*Marasca* cherries if you can find them, otherwise use Morelos or Bings)
- ½ cup demerara sugar
- ½ cup water
- 1 vanilla bean
- 1 cup Maraschino liqueur

Steps

1. Remove stems and pits from the cherries. I recommend pitting the cherries in a large storage plastic bag to avoid splattering cherry juice all over the place.
2. Split the vanilla bean and scrape the seeds.
3. Place sugar, water, vanilla bean and vanilla seeds in a saucepan over medium heat and bring to a boil.
4. Lower the heat and simmer for 5 minutes (stirring occasionally).
5. Take the pan off the heat and let cool fully.
6. Strain the liquid into a container.
7. Stir in the maraschino liqueur.
8. Place the cherries in a 1-quart jar and pour in the liquid (syrup and liqueur) .
9. Cover tightly and store in a cool dark place.
10. Wait at least three weeks before using (this is the hardest step!).

Variations

- Some people suggest blanching the cherries in boiling salted water for 4 minutes, then rinsing in cold water to get rid of the salt (after step 1). This will not make the cherries salty. The theory is that the salt draws out water from the cherries, which enables them to keep a firm texture. The boiling also stops enzymatic reactions and destroys yeasts that may ferment the fruit. If you decide to do this, make sure you do not over-blanch (you don't want to cook the cherries).
- Another option is to add the pits to the steeping liquid. This will add a special "almondy", slightly bitter flavor to the product, which some enjoy. If you use this option, keep the pits after pitting, place them in a bag, smash them with a mallet, and add them to the saucepan along with the syrup and vanilla.
- I purposely kept the base recipe fairly simple with just vanilla. But feel free to experiment with other spices based on your taste. Common choices are star anise, cinnamon, cloves, allspice, nutmeg, cardamom and anise seeds.
- To help the cherries keep a deep red color, you can add a concentrated hibiscus tea or some beets to the jar.
- Using Maraschino liqueur as suggested in the recipe will yield an authentic-tasting Maraschino cherry. But Maraschino liqueur is not to everyone's taste. You can substitute – at least partially – brandy, rum or bourbon (or a combination) for the Maraschino liqueur.
- If you want more cherry flavor, you can also add some cherry juice (or substitute juice for the water when making the syrup). You can make your own cherry juice by processing pitted cherries in a blender with water (½ cup water per pound of cherries), then straining.
- Sweetness is also a very personal choice. Personally, I don't like my cherries too sweet, but if you do, feel free to increase the amount of syrup.

Cherries Brûlées

You can set your cherries on fire in order to release interesting flavors and aromas. The flavors are even more intense if you use some bitters along with the sugar.

1. Put Maraschino cherries in a glass (make sure the glass is tempered so it can take the heat).
2. Sprinkle some white sugar on top.
3. Put Angostura bitters in an atomizer bottle.
4. Spray Angostura bitters on the cherries and sugar and over the inside of the glass.
5. Light a match, lighter or torch and hold over glass.
6. Spray Angostura bitters through the flame and into the glass. This will spark a flame and light the Angostura in the glass on fire.
7. Spritz more angostura in the glass (about 10 sprays) until all the sugar is caramelized.
8. Let the glass cool.
9. Build the cocktail on top of the cherries.
10. You can also muddle the cherries a little to release their flavor.
11. Shake and serve

Instead of building the drink on top, you can also prepare the cherries in advanced this way and use them in drinks or on skewers on top of a drink.

Dropped Cherries

The easiest way to use cherries is to simply drop them in the drink.

Depending on the consistency of the drink, they may sink in the liquid or, if the glass is packed with ice or topped with cream or foam, they can rest on top.

Cherries on a Stick

Another simple way to introduce cherries is to slide them on a cocktail stick (or a piece of skewer) and drop the stick in the drink.

Traditionally, we use an odd number of cherries; one or three in practice, as five seems overly greedy (though it is very tempting). But if you use two, the cherry police won't come after you. You can also hang the stick on the rim of the glass (dangling from the top cherry), or lay it flat on top of the drink.

Hanging on the Rim

You can cut a small slit at the bottom of the cherry and slide it on the rim of the glass.

Note that, in this case, you can use a fresh cherry and even include the stem for a little extra flair.

Muddling

You can muddle the cherries in the bottom of the glass before pouring the drink. This will release the flavors of the cherry into the drink. The appearance can be a

bit hit-or-miss, as sometimes there are attractive pieces of cherries floating in the drink, while other times the bits of cherry look messy. An alternative is to cut the cherries neatly with a knife and strategically position them in the drink.

Cherry Flowers

Here's a simple but attractive garnish made by cutting a cherry's top into segments and spreading them out to give the illusion of a flower. Adding a sprig of mint or two adds a nice contrast.

1. Remove the stem from the cherry (if using fresh cherries).
2. Place the cherry on cutting board.
3. Slice through the top of the cherry with a paring knife to create 6 sections.
5. Separate the "petals" a little using the tip of your knife.
6. Float on top of the drink (optionally adding a sprig of mint).

In Combination

Cherries are often used in combination with other fruits such as oranges or pineapple in what is known as a "flag" or a "boat".

These are covered in detail in chapter 5.

You can also cut the strawberry in half to reveal its interior (some have interesting internal patterns).

For drinks with ice all the way to the top, you can cut a few slices and fan them out on top.

STRAWBERRIES

Strawberries are not often used as garnishes, mainly because of the cost and the limited options to serve them. But they are used for a few drinks such as Strawberry Daiquiris, Mimosas and sometimes with a glass of Champagne.

Basic Garnishes

The easiest way to use a strawberry as a garnish is to simply cut a slit at the bottom and place it on the rim of the glass. Or for a slightly different look, you can cut the slit on the side so the strawberry hangs at an angle or even horizontally.

Strawberry Rose

For a more ambitious garnish, you can turn the strawberry into a rose.

1. Holding the strawberry leaf-side-down, mentally divide it into quarters. Cut a slit in the flesh near the base on one section (be careful to not slice off the section completely).
2. Pull the knife away from the strawberry a little to separate the section from the fruit.
3. Repeat for the other three sides.
4. Cut a similar slit higher than the previous ones and offset from the ones below.
5. Repeat for the other three sides.
6. Create a third layer of similar slits offset from the layer below.
7. Cut a slit at the tip of the berry.
8. Cut a slit at the bottom of the strawberry through the leaves. Leave the knife in the slit.
9. Attach to the glass sliding the knife off the slit.
10. Using the tip of your knife, gently pull out the "petals".

LYCHEES

For the purpose of garnishing, you can use the lychee the same way you may use an olive: drop one in the drink or place a few on a cocktail stick. Of course, you would use this garnish for cocktails that contain lychee juice or liqueur and for Asian-inspired cocktails where the lychee might provide a nice complement.

RED CURRANTS

Red currants can provide a simple but very attractive garnish.
The most obvious way to use them is hanging them from the rim, but you could also float a few in the drink.

BLUEBERRIES

Blueberries provide a pretty versatile garnish.

The most common way they are used is simply dropping them in the drink, either on top or pushing them down into the drink and scattering them (assuming it contains ice). They can also be skewered and laid on top of the glass.

They are sometimes used in combination with other fruits.

OTHER BERRIES

Berries are pretty fragile so you need to handle them with care.

The most common way to use them is to skewer a few (of potentially different varieties) on a cocktail stick and drop it in the drink or lay it across the top of the glass.

You can also use a branch of rosemary as a skewer.

COBBLERS

One of my favorite ways to decorate a drink is with fresh fruit, and particularly berries. This is not commonly seen these days, but it used to be very popular. There is actually an old family of drinks called "cobblers", which are essentially tall drinks (usually with a fortified wine like Sherry as a base) served in a glass with crushed ice and topped with pieces of fruit.

Created in the 1830s, the Sherry Cobbler was the most popular drink of the late 1800s. Besides being a delicious drink, it had several things going for it at the time. The fruit definitely added to the visual appeal, but even more important to its success was the use of two novel items that we now take for granted: ice and a straw (which at the time was most likely a reed or hollow pasta).

Here's a recipe for the traditional Sherry Cobbler:

1. Shake 4 oz of Sherry (dry *fino* or the sweeter and mellower *Amontillado*), 2 orange slices and 2 teaspoons of sugar with ice.

2. Pour unstrained into a tall glass.

3. Add crushed ice if necessary so the glass is 80% full (it will make a sturdy base for the fruit).

4. Top with fresh berries.

5. Insert straw.

The Sherry Cobbler is a particularly pleasant and light drink with sweet sherry flavors brightened by the zesty taste of orange.

Over the years, there have been many variations on the Sherry cobbler. For instance, you can substitute Bourbon for the Sherry and use a bar spoonful of Maraschino liqueur instead of the orange. Feel free to experiment with other spirits such as brandy, rum or even gin.

Don't feel that you are restricted to these classic cobbler recipes either. I am only mentioning them to give you some historical context, but I encourage you to use cobbler-style fresh fruit toppings on other drinks you create.

Make sure you use fresh-looking and in-season fruits (eg: raspberries in the summer, cranberries in the fall, etc). Also, as usual, pay attention to the flavors of the drink itself, and choose fruits that complement the drink. Finally, pay close attention to the way you arrange the fruit. Use a combination of 2 or 3 different types of fruit and arrange them in a pleasing and artistic manner. Don't just plop them haphazardly on top of the ice.

ICE BOWL

You can also present berries in a small ice bowl as described in chapter 8.

35

Chapter 3 – Apples

This chapter will offer a few interesting ways to garnish with apples from the basic wedge to fans and more sophisticated offset wedges.

It goes without saying that a piece of apple is the perfect garnish for drinks containing apple flavors such as those based on Applejack, Calvados or Apple Schnapps.

Note that apples will brown if left exposed to the air, so I recommend making the garnishes as needed. If you must make them ahead of time, keep them in acidulated water (i.e water that contains either lemon or lime juice).

WHEEL

The simplest way to garnish with apples is to cut it into wheels, either vertically for a flat look (a), or horizontally for a nice star pattern in the center (b). Cut a slit in it and hang on the rim or float the wheel.

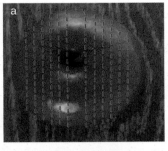 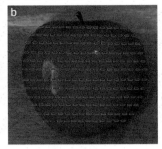

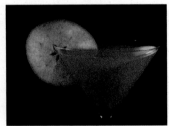 

SLICE

The slice is another classic apple cut which is used as the base for a number of garnishes.

1. Cut an apple in half vertically.
2. Lay the halves flat and cut in half again.
3. Cut the center part of each quarter at a 45 degree angle to remove the core and end bits.
4. Cut the cored quarter in slices.
5. Cut a slit on the slice and hang on the glass.

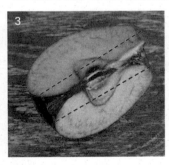 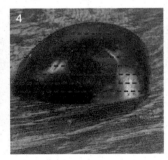

 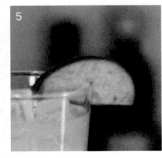

You can cut the slit to have the wedge face in or out, up or down, straight or at an angle. Here are a couple of examples.

FAN

For a more interesting look, skewer a few slices on a cocktail stick and fan them out a little.

1. Cut 4 slices out of a wedge.
2. Stack the 4 slices and cut the edges to even them out.
3. Secure with a cocktail stick and fan the slices out.
4. Rest both sides of the cocktail stick and the lower slice on top of the glass.

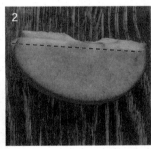 

Variations

Using a paring knife, cut a curved sliver from the edge of the stacked slices. This will give it a shape close to a leaf.

You have a few options as to how to place the stick: it can be either laid on top of the glass (with a slice resting on the rim) and dipped into the drink.

Here are a few examples.

6. Using a melon baller, cut out a half-sphere from the reserved piece of apple.
7. Create a notch on the round side of the half-sphere by pushing it (not too hard) on the rim of the glass.
8. Remove the half-sphere from the glass and attach its flat side to the toothpick.
9. Position the assembly on the glass.
10. Fan out the slices.
11. Attach a cherry on top.

Option: instead of using the half-sphere, you can balance the assembly on the rim.

CRESCENT FAN

This is similar to the previous garnish, but this time the slices are cut in a crescent shape.

1. Cut 4 thin slices from an apple.
2. Stack the slices.
3. Cut an oblong shape from the inner side to form a crescent.
4. Place a cocktail stick through the slices at one end.
5. Offset the slices a little.
6. Drop in drink with slices resting on the rim.

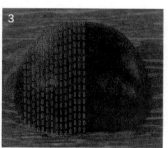

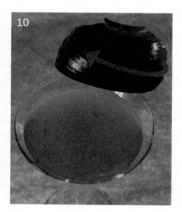

SPIRAL STAIRCASE

This garnish takes the idea of the fan to the nth degree to give the impression of a spiral staircase.

1. Cut an apple vertically ½" from the center.
2. Place the cut piece flat on your board, with the part that was the top of the apple facing you.
3. Cut thin slices from half of the piece. Reserve the other half.
4. Reassemble the slices and line them up.
5. Pierce the assembly with a toothpick vertically and facing up.

Cherry

Offset Wedge

This garnish takes the simple apple wedge to the next level. It involves cutting a V shape out of the top and offsetting it a bit.

1. Place an apple wedge flat on a board.
2. Make a cut parallel to the top side, but do not cut all the way through.
3. Turn the wedge over and make a similar cut parallel to the top side (again do not cut all the way through).
4. Pull the center part out, leaving a V-shape wedge.
5. Place the center part back in but slightly offset.
6. Cut a slit in the outer wedge, at a 45 degrees angle. You may need to cut twice removing a tiny sliver of apple in order for the slit to be a large enough.
7. Place on rim.

Triple-Offset Wedge

This builds on the previous technique. It involves cutting V shapes of increasingly smaller size and re-assembling them in a staggered fashion.

1. Place an apple wedge flat on a board.
2. Make a cut parallel to the top side, but do not cut all the way through.
3. Turn the wedge over and make a similar cut parallel to the top side (again do not cut all the way through).
4. Pull the center part out leaving you with a V-shape wedge.
5. Repeat steps 2-4 with the part you removed from the center.
6. Repeat steps 2-4 with the smaller part you removed from the center in step 5.
7. Reassemble the parts with a small offset between the each section.
8. Cut a slit in the outer wedge, at a 45 degrees angle. You may need to cut twice removing a tiny sliver of apple in order for the slit to be a large enough.
9. Place on rim.

Symmetric Offset Wedge

Along the same theme as the previous garnish, this technique involves cutting increasingly smaller V shapes from a wedge. The difference is that the inner Vs are split and offset creating a symmetrical pattern in the middle of it.

1. Place an apple wedge flat on a board.
2. Make a cut parallel to the top side, but do not cut all the way through.
3. Turn the wedge over and make a similar cut parallel to the top side (again do not cut all the way through).
4. Pull the center part out leaving a V-shape wedge.
5. Repeat steps 2-4 with the part you removed from the center.
6. Repeat steps 2-4 with the smaller part you removed from the center in step 5.
7. Reassemble all parts except the outermost wedge.
8. Cut assembly in half.
9. Offset the center pieces in each half.
10. Place each half in the outermost wedge and offset them slightly.
11. Cut a slit in the outermost wedge.
12. Hang on glass.

Chapter 4 – Other Fruits

This chapter will discuss garnishes from various other types of fruit that have not been covered thus far.

In particular, we will look at pineapples, bananas, coconuts, melons, star fruits, kumquats, kiwis and pears.

PINEAPPLES

Pineapples are less frequently used as a garnish, and are mostly relegated to tiki-style or tropical drinks (the Piña Colada and the Mai Tai being the better known ones). Even though they are edible, they are mainly used for visual appeal. They can be used individually, but are often combined with a cherry or other fruit to make a flag (see chapter 5).

Pineapples will dry out, so do not make your garnishes too long in advance, and if you do, make sure they are kept in an airtight container.

Wedges

The most common pineapple garnish is the wedge.
1. Cut off the base and top. Reserve the top as the leaves can be used in garnishes (see next page).
2. Cut in half lengthwise (vertically).
3. Lay each piece flat, and cut in half (making quarters), then in half again (making eighths).
4. Keeping 4 eighths held together, cut ¾" slices, perpendicular to the previous cuts, creating wedges.
5. Cut a slit in the flesh of each wedge. Depending on the look you're after, you can cut the sli at the point or on the edge (in which case the wedge will rest at an angle on the glass).
6. Hang on rim.

Spears

The spear provides a slightly more sophisticated garnish than the wedge.

1. Cut the base and top off. Reserve the top as the leaves can be used in garnishes (see next page).
2. Cut the skin off the pineapple. Make sure you remove the eyes as well, but do not cut off too much of the flesh. You can always come back later and remove more eyes.
3. Cut in half lengthwise (vertically).
4. Lay each piece flat and cut in half (making quarters).
5. Cut off the core.
6. Cut each piece in three lengthwise again.
7. Cut down to size based on the size of your glass.
8. Place vertically in the drink.

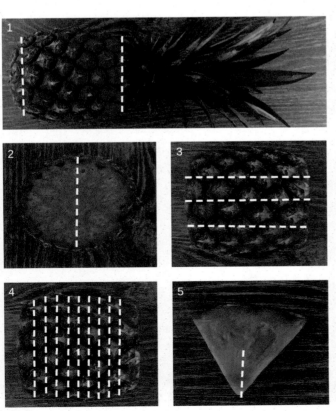

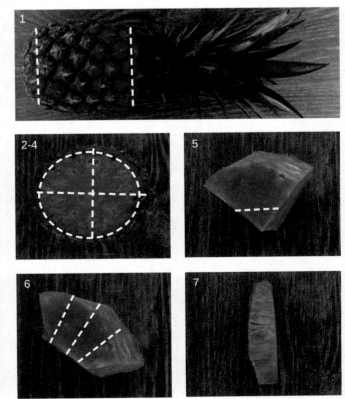

Moon

This garnish takes the shape of a crescent moon for a more whimsical look.
1. Select a small pineapple.
2. Cut out a slice.
3. Using a cookie cutter or a cocktail shaker tin, cut out a section of the slice to make a crescent shape.
4. Cut a vertical slit in the crescent.
5. Slide the slit onto the glass (crescent facing out).

Variation

You can attach a berry or cherry on the inside of a crescent with a toothpick.

Using Leaves

The pineapple leaves can be used on their own or to add a bit of flair to other garnishes. That's why I suggested in the preceding sections to not discard the top. Make sure you choose nice looking leaves, and wash them thoroughly.

You can just drop a leaf in the drink for a minimalist look; or you can take 2-3 leaves and pin them together with a toothpick and stagger them slightly. You can also combine a wedge and leaves by cutting a slit into the rind and sliding some trimmed leaves into it.

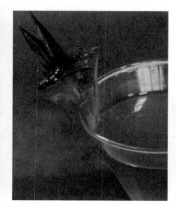

Flag

Flags are covered in more detail in chapter 5, but here's a simple example of making a flag from pineapple and a cherry.

1. Cut a slice out of the center of a pineapple.
2. Cut the slice in half.
3. Cut each half in thirds to make triangles.
4. Cut a slit at the bottom of the triangle.
5. Pick 2 or 3 leaves from the pineapple.
6. Stack the leaves, and trim the ends to even them out and make a point.
7. Trim the bottom white part of the leaves.
8. Fan out the 3 leaves slightly.
9. Secure with a toothpick and attach to the side of the pineapple triangle.
10. Attach a cherry to the toothpick and trim the pick.
11. Place on glass using the slit.

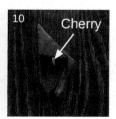

Cherry

BANANAS

Bananas are generally used only in banana-based cocktails, where most of the fruit is used in the drink and some is saved for decoration. Note that bananas will discolor if left out, so use them immediately after cutting.

Slice

The most obvious garnish is to simply cut a slit in a banana slice and hang it on the rim of the glass.

Some people like to keep the skin on the slice in order to give the garnish more sturdiness.

Caramelized Bananas

For a more interesting look, you can caramelize one side of the slice, and place it across the rim using a cocktail stick.

1. Cut a peeled banana in ½" slices.
2. Place on an aluminum-foil-covered cookie sheet.
3. Sprinkle sugar evenly on the slices.
4. Light a small propane torch (as used to make crème brûlée) and set to low flame.
5. Run the flame over the sugar. Do not stay too long in one spot. Instead, make back and forth movements until the sugar is caramelized.
6. Let cool.
7. Place the slice on a cocktail stick or skewer that is wide enough to span the mouth of the glass.
8. Place on top of the glass.

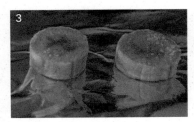

Dolphin

For a very *tiki-esque* (some will call it cheesy or corny) look, you can turn half a banana into a dolphin. You will need a banana, a piece of orange skin, a toothpick and a grape.

1. Cut the banana in half and keep the half with the stem.
2. Cut the tip off the stem to even it out.
3. Slice through the stem and a third of the way through the banana.
4. Using a paring knife, cut two small circles from an orange skin (remove excess pith).
5. Cut the ends off a toothpick and pierce each orange circle with them.
6. Attach the orange "eyes" to the banana.
7. Cut a slit at the bottom of the banana.
8. Part the stem and place a grape in the mouth of the dolphin.
9. Slide slit on glass or tiki mug.

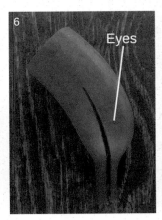

Eyes

STAR FRUIT

Like the banana, the star fruit can just be sliced and perched on the glass, or they can simply be floated on the drink. You can also put one on a cocktail stick and place the stick across the top of the glass. Because of its interesting shape, it does bring a certain elegance as a garnish.

COCONUT

Coconuts are not a common garnish item, but can work well with tropical-influenced cocktails and of course those that contain Malibu or other coconut-flavored ingredients.

Flakes

Coconut flakes can be sprinkled on top the drink. For a more interesting flavor, toast the coconut flakes first by spreading the flakes on a cookie sheet, and baking at 350ºF for 7-8 minutes, or until golden brown.

Curl

For a minimalist almost zen-like garnish, you can use a simple coconut curl hanging from the rim.

1. Split coconut open and remove interior flesh.
2. Slice off thin strips of coconut using a peeler.
3. Roll strip and hold to give it a curl.
4. Hang on rim.

Rim

Coconut flakes can also be used as a rimming ingredient (see chapter 7 for details).

MELON

The melon garnish is the perfect accompaniment to a Midori-based drink.

Balls

Using a melon baller, cut out small spheres of melon, and drop or skewer them as described in the olive section (see chapter 6).

For a more interesting look, mix and match different colors of melon (for instance a green melon, a cantaloupe and/or a watermelon).

Also experiment intermixing melon balls with other fruit and even small leaves and flowers as in the example below.

Wedge

Cut a thin wedge of melon, cut a slit in the flesh and hang it on the rim.

The slit can be cut in various positions and at different angles depending on how you want the wedge to hang on the glass.

Finally, try pinning together some melon balls with a small wedge of skin for contrast, as in this example which uses watermelon.

A slice of kumquat can be treated as a small citrus slice and hung on the rim. But since they are so small , it is also possible to hang them whole on the rim of the glass (optionally keeping their leaves).

Alternatively, float a few slices on top of a drink or push them into the drink and disperse them.

They can also be displayed on a cocktail stick like you would olives (use slices, half or whole kumquats).

For an unusual look, cut off the edge of the kiwi slice to create a square. The contrast of the square edge with the circular center provides an interesting appearance.

PEARS

You can use pears in much the same way you would use apples (see chapter 3). The following example illustrates a pear fan (with a few blueberries thrown in for color contrast).

KIWIS

Kiwis provide another great opportunity to add visual contrast to a drink. Their green color complements nicely a variety of cocktail colors.

Like other round fruits, kiwis can be sliced and perched on the rim of the glass or plunged into the drink. This picture illustrates both options.

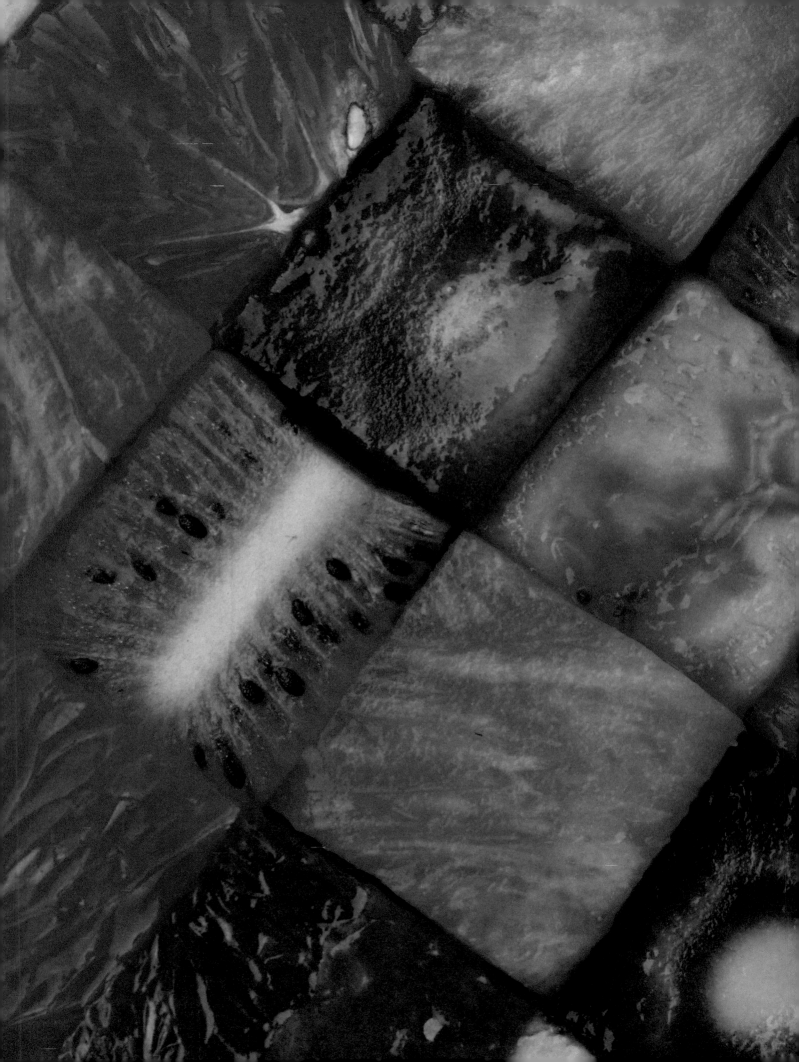

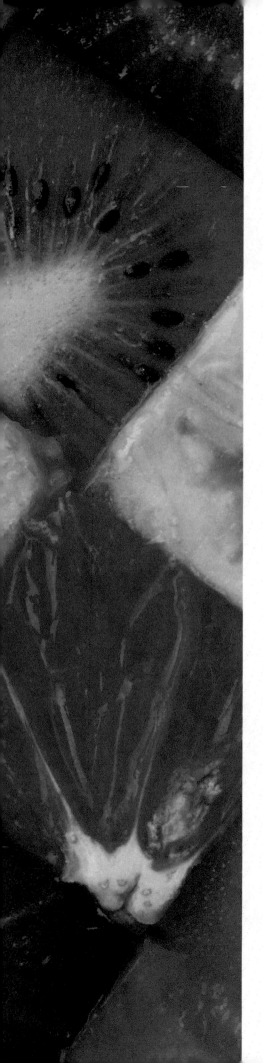

Chapter 5 – Multi-fruit Garnishes

In this chapter, we discuss garnishes made of combinations of different fruits.

In particular we will cover skewers, flags, boats and variations thereof.

We then move on to more advanced garnishes that are very impressive but do require a bit more time to prepare.

SKEWERING

One of the easiest multi-item garnishes you can make is to simply pin a few pieces of fruit together with a small skewer or cocktail stick. The skewer can either be dropped into the drink or balanced on top of the glass.

It is usually more appealing to have an odd number of items. Sometimes one is enough, especially if you're going for the minimalist look.

Three is typically the right number. The classic example is the three olives on a cocktail stick dropped into a martini.

Five items tend to be overwhelming unless the items are relatively small (like blueberries).

As usual it is best to match the items to the flavors in the drink. For instance, if melon flavor (eg: Midori) is prominent in the drink, you may want to make melon balls, skewer them and place them over or in the drink. Using different color melons improves the visual appeal.

Add variety by using different types of fruits on one skewer.

Feel free to create asymmetric design by using two pieces of one type of fruit and one of another, of perhaps different sizes or of increasing size.

You can stand your skewer or cocktail stick vertically for a more architectural garnish. This will work for drinks packed with ice where you can lodge the skewer between ice cubes. You may want to serve the drink with a straw so that the guest does not poke his eye out when drinking...

You can also interweave herbs, leaves and/or tiny flowers between fruits.

Get creative with your skewers. For instance, why not use a sturdy herb like rosemary as a skewer. Or perhaps use a cinnamon stick or a sugar cane spear.

As we get into variations of flags and boats, the line between the two blurs. Don't let the terminology hold you back. You can call your garnish whatever you like as long as it's attractive and complements your drink well.

A variety of fruits can be used with these techniques, but the most common involve a maraschino cherry (see chapter 2 for tips on buying or making quality cherries).

Orange/Cherry Flag

The most common flag uses a cherry and orange half-wheel.

1. Start with an orange half-wheel (see chapter 1).
2. Push a toothpick or cocktail stick through a cherry.
3. Holding the orange slice between index finger and thumb, place the tip of the cocktail stick on top of the orange slice (on the peel side).
4. Push the cocktail stick through the orange peel and into the flesh (but not all the way through the edge of the slice). Be careful to keep the stick straight otherwise it will poke out the side of the orange wheel.
5. Cut a ¼" deep slit in the orange slice at the desired angle (based on the orientation you desire on the glass).
6. Slide slit onto rim of glass.

FLAGS AND BOATS

Flags and boats are an excellent and easy way to jazz up your garnishes. They involve stacking several pieces of fruit in a given configuration and securing them with a toothpick.

Flags are generally made by pinning a cherry to another piece of fruit (such as a pineapple wedge or orange half-wheel) and placing on the glass rim. Flags are the typical garnish for a Tom Collins, Whiskey Sour, Amaretto Sour and many tropical drinks.

Boats are usually made by folding a citrus wheel around a cherry (taco-style), and pinning them in that shape with a toothpick. They typically float on the drink, or are partially sunk, usually resting against the rim. They are often used on frothy or creamy cocktails.

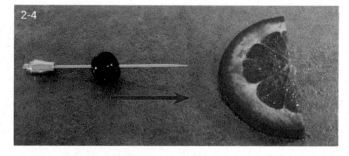

Variations

Some people prefer to pin the cherry to the side of the slice rather than the top. This is less commonly used, but a valid choice.

The cherry can also be attached at the end of the wedge in a more vertical arrangement.

Another option is to place the cherry on the flesh side of the slice. In this case, you probably need to pierce through the cherry fully, otherwise it might fall off. You can even cut out a slot about the size of the cherry in the orange slice and place the cherry in the slot.

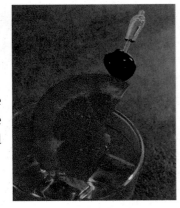

so that the toothpick will go in more easily.

5. Cut a ½" deep slit in the pineapple flesh at the desired angle (based on the orientation you desire on the glass).
6. Slide the slit onto the rim of the glass.

Flag Variations

Don't feel like you're limited to the classic orange/cherry or pineapple/cherry combinations. Experiment making flags with other fruits such as bananas, kiwis, strawberries, raspberries, etc. In particular, if your drink is based on a particular fruit flavor, it would make sense to include that fruit in the flag.

There's also no reason why you can't have more than two pieces of fruits pinned together. Try different combination, but keep in mind the flavors of the cocktail, so that the garnish does not appear disconnected from the general profile of the drink.

Finally, you can get creative with the relative positioning of the fruits. Here are some examples to get you started, but this is not an exhaustive list, and the options are only limited by your imagination.

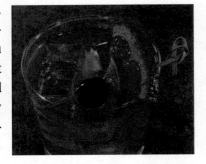

Here I stacked a cherry on top of a lime wheel, attached them with a cocktail pick and placed the wheel horizontally over the drink with the wheel balanced over the edge.

Pineapple/Cherry Flag

Another common flag uses a pineapple wedge and a cherry. The technique is similar to the one explained for the orange and cherry flag.

1. Cut a small pineapple wedge (see chapter 4).
2. Push a toothpick or cocktail stick through a cherry.
3. Holding the pineapple wedge between index finger and thumb, place the tip of the cocktail stick on top of the pineapple (on the skin side).
4. Push the cocktail stick through the skin of the pineapple wedge and into the flesh (but not all the way through the edge of the wedge). If your cocktail stick is made of metal or sturdy material, you will have no problem piercing the skin of the pineapple as described, but if you're using a flimsy toothpick, you may need to poke a hole into the pineapple first,

The pieces of fruit could also be pinned sideways. This example uses the leaves of a pineapple for variety of both color and shape.

Finally, here's another example of stacking that produces a simple yet elegant garnish. Skewer a couple of small berries (such as red currants or cranberries) on a cocktail stick and insert in a citrus wedge which you then perch on the glass with a slit as usual or between the skin and the flesh.

Why not stack items vertically as in the following example. It could even be topped with a little umbrella to complete the tropical (some will call it corny) look.

Cherry-Lime "C"

Here's another option which uses a lime peel and a cherry. The peel is curved in a C shape and the cherry sits in the middle of it.

1. Cut a ½" wheel out of a lime.
2. Using a paring knife, separate the flesh from the skin.
3. Cut about ¼ of the peel away to create the C shape.
4. Pierce the bottom part of the C with a skewer.

5. Place the cherry in the middle of the C and pierce with the toothpick.
6. Continue the toothpick's upward motion piercing the lime skin that creates the top of the C.
7. Place the assembly on the drink.

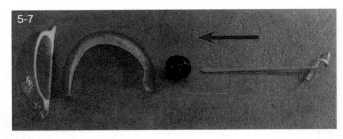

Tropical Bird Tail

Here is a variation of a pineapple/cherry flag, where the pineapple piece is cut out of the top of the fruit, creating a dangling tropical bird "tail". This one has a real tiki feel to it as well, and would be happier on a tiki mug than a dainty coupe...

1. Cut the top of a pineapple (1 inch below the leaves).
2. Cut the top in half vertically.
3. Lay each piece flat on a board and cut in half, then in half again (making eighths).
4. Cut a slit in the flesh at an angle.
5. Attach a cherry to the top of the pineapple piece with a toothpick.
6. Slide the piece on a tiki mug using the slit.

Sailboat

This garnish feels right at home on top of a tiki mug. It stacks a lemon wedge, orange peel and cherry in a construction that looks somewhat like a sailboat. Note that we're starting to deviate quite a bit from the basic flag here, but I include this example in this section to inspire you to stack fruits in ingenious combinations.

1. Cut a 1" wheel out of an orange.
2. Using a paring knife, separate the flesh from the skin.
3. Cut about ¼ of the peel away (creating a C shape).
4. Cut a lemon wedge.
5. Spear a cherry with a toothpick.
6. Push the toothpick through both sides of the orange "C".
7. Push the toothpick into the lemon wedge.
8. Place the assembly over a narrow glass or tiki mug.

Orange and Cherry Boat

The most common type of boat uses an orange slice and a cherry. It is very easy and simply involves pinning a cherry in the middle of a curved orange slice.

1. Slice a wheel out of an orange.
2. Pierce the orange wheel with a cocktail pick and attach a cherry to it.
3. Push the toothpick through the other side of the orange wheel, folding it taco-style. This will keep the cherry secured and maintain the fold of the wheel.
4. Place the boat on top of the drink (resting the cocktail stick on the rim).

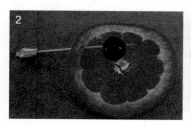 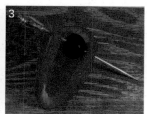

Variations

Don't feel restricted to the orange/cherry combination. You can use a variety of fruits (whatever *floats your boat*).

You can also keep the wheel flatter, place smaller fruit (such as pomegranate seeds or cranberries) and maybe a mint leaf or two on top, and lay the cocktail stick across the glass.

Instead of laying the boat flat on the drink, why not hang it vertically by placing both sides of the cocktail stick on the rim of the glass.

Attach a cherry or raspberry on the outside of the folded wheel, secure with a cocktail stick through the top of the fold, and lay across the glass or in the drink.

Boats on Narrow Glasses

Boats can sometimes be too big for the glass (especially if using oranges). This causes the garnish to look unbalanced and out of proportion.

To solve this, you can choose to use a smaller fruit (assuming compatibility of flavors) or place the boat vertically as described above.

Also consider serving the drink with a straw if the garnish still takes too much space.

Finally, you can cut a slit in the wheel and overlap the sides before securing with the cocktail stick (as in this example).

This will create an interesting concave shape that adds a third dimension to the garnish and takes less space .

CHERRY IN APPLE

Here's an interesting multi-fruit garnish combining an apple slice and a cherry, but instead of pinning them side-by-side as you would with a flag, you carve a hole on the apple slice, and insert the cherry in it.

1. Cut a ½" slice out of an apple.
2. Lay the slice flat on a board and cut a hole the size of a cherry towards one edge.
3. Cut a slit on the opposite side.
4. Insert a cherry in the cut circle. The cherry will protrude a little on each side.
5. Slide the slice on the glass.

TWISTED BOAT

This variation on a boat provides a more interesting look than the standard "fold". The slice is cut and folded on itself in both directions to create a twisted pattern. A cherry is usually inserted in the top fold.

1. Start with an orange wheel.
2. Cut a slit from one edge to the middle of the wheel.
3. Fold the wheel in half.
4. Fold one side of the slit in and the other out.
5. Insert a cherry in the top fold.
6. Secure with a cocktail stick going through all four layers.
7. Drop in the drink.

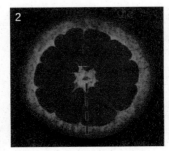
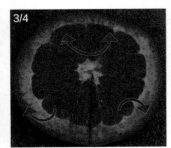

Variations

- You can insert 2 cherries, one in each fold of the wheel.
- Use different fruits. For instance use raspberries instead of cherries.
- Attach the cherry on the outside of the twisted citrus wheel, and hang in on the glass by the cherry or lay it across the glass.
    1. Follow steps 1-3 of the previous garnish.
    2. Thread a cherry on a cocktail stick.
    3. Pierce the cocktail stick through all the layers of the folded wheel.
    4. Hang across the rim of the glass.

CITRUS PEEL & CHERRY WIGGLE

This garnish differs from the previous ones in this section in that it uses a piece of citrus peel, instead of a wheel. The swath is curved in an S shape with cherries in the folds.

1. Cut a swath out of a citrus peel (see page 22-24).
2. Lay the peel on a board and even out to a rectangle.

3. Wrap a cherry in the peel on one side and secure with a cocktail stick.
4. Place the cherry on the stick, wrap the peel around it and attach it to the stick.
5. Repeat step 4 with the 3rd cherry.
6. Place on top of the glass or drop in the drink.

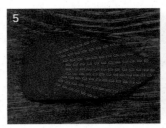
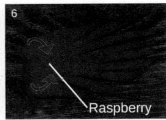

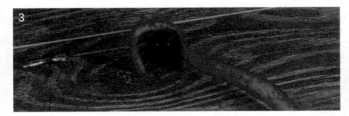

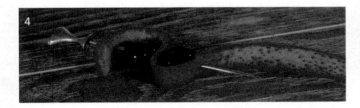

Variation: For a simpler garnish, use a shorter citrus peel, make only 2 folds and use only 2 cherries.

Citrus Burst

Here's a pretty (albeit a bit more advanced) garnish using a lemon peel and a raspberry. The cuts need to be precise for the garnish to look even, so use a sharp knife and take your time.

1. Cut the skin off a quarter of a lemon.
2. Lay the skin flat, yellow side on the board.
3. Keeping the knife horizontal, cut the pith off the skin (see tips on page 23).
4. Turn the skin over (yellow side up).
5. Cut slits as illustrated in figure 5.
6. Place a raspberry at the bottom of the prepared lemon skin and fold the lemon around it.
7. Secure with a cocktail stick sideways.
8. Place on top of the drink with the lemon "fringes" hanging over the sides of the glass.

Raspberry

Citrus Burst 2

This garnish is in the same vein as the previous one, using a carved citrus peel jutting out with a raspberry in the middle. The carving is a bit more complex and requires more precision. But it looks daintier and more elegant.

1. Cut the skin off a quarter orange wedge.
2. Laying the skin flat on the board, cut off the pith.
3. Turn the skin over (orange side up).
4. Cut the end off on one side to create a straight edge.
5. Make slits as per figure 5 to create four points.
6. For each point, remove an oblong section as per figure 6.
7. Place a raspberry in the center of the uncut part of the orange skin.
8. Slide a cocktail stick through the side to secure all parts.
9. Place on the drink.

Chapter 6 – Savory Garnishes

This chapter is dedicated to savory garnishes. These are less common but include some emblematic items such as olives (for martinis) and cocktail onions (for Gibsons).

Included in this chapter are garnishes made of cucumber, celery and carrots. We also cover the use of herbs, spices and edible flowers as decoration, as well as garnishing with bacon and jerky.

Finally, we discuss a disturbing trend which involves piling insane amounts of food on top of a Bloody Mary.

OLIVES

Olives have been cultivated for over 5,000 years and have been a staple of numerous cuisines. In the cocktail world, even though they are used in only a couple of drinks (notably the Martini and the Bloody Mary), the olive is an iconic garnish.

There are a number of quality brands of olives suitable for cocktails. The most commonly used varieties are *Castelvetrano*, *Cerignola*, and *Kalamata*. They are sometimes stuffed with pimiento (a pickled pepper), almonds, anchovies, cheese, etc. Personally, being a bit of a purist, I prefer my olives "unstuffed", especially since sometimes the contents of the olive ooze into the drink, imparting a weird flavor and often a less than appetizing appearance. Look for olives that are pitted, as serving an unpitted olive could end up being awkward for the guest (ranging from an embarrassing spit-out to a choking hazard). Make sure you keep the olives in the fridge before serving, otherwise they will warm up the drink.

You can simply drop one olive or spear one or three of them (two is against tradition) on a cocktail stick.

COCKTAIL ONIONS

Cocktail onions are made from pearl onions (a small, mild flavored onion), pickled in a tangy, salty brine. They are rarely used as a garnish. The only drink of note that uses them is the Gibson (essentially a martini served with an onion instead of an olive).

Most liquor stores (and even some grocery stores) carry pickled onions, but it's easy to make your own. Below is a recipe adapted from Todd Thrasher's recipe, published in *Imbibe*. His version was a bit too sweet for my taste, so mine includes a lot less sugar (but feel free to adjust to your own taste).

Ingredients

- 1 lb pearl onions (fresh ones are sometimes hard to find, so you can use frozen ones if necessary)
- 4 cups white wine vinegar
- 3 cups warm water
- ½ cup sugar
- 2 tablespoons kosher salt
- 1 tablespoon pickling spices (found in the canning section of the grocery store)

Steps

1. Peel the onions (if using frozen onions, that step is already done for you).
2. Combine vinegar, water, sugar and salt in a saucepan.
3. Heat on a low heat, and stir until dissolved.
4. Place spices in a spice bag (you can make one out of cheesecloth) and add to the saucepan.
5. Add the onions to the saucepan (ensuring all are covered with liquid).
6. Bring to a boil, and boil for 1 minute (do not exceed a minute, otherwise the onions will lose their crunch).
7. Remove from the heat.
8. Let cool to room temperature.
9. Transfer the onions and liquid to glass jars.
10. Keep refrigerated for up to two months.

Cucumbers

Cucumbers are also rarely used as a garnish and seem to only make sense if the drink has a strong cucumber flavor. Here are a few options on how to use them as a garnish.

Tip

If you prepare your cucumber garnishes ahead of time, keep them in cold water so that they stay fresh.

Slice

Like other slices, cucumber slices can be hung on the glass or floated on top of the drink. If you choose the floating option, keep in mind the cucumber will contribute some sourness to the drink the longer it stays in there.

For a more interesting look, score the cucumber (using a channel knife) before slicing it. See instructions for notched citrus wheels (chapter 1).

Spear

Another simple way to garnish with a cucumber is to cut it into a spear.

Cut the cucumber in eighths lengthwise (or smaller depending on its girth), and cut to a length appropriate for your glass, so that it protrudes an inch or so above the rim.

Ribbon

The ribbon is a simple but elegant way to dress a cocktail. It takes the form of a wiggle made from a thin strip of cucumber and is secured with a toothpick. You can drop it in the drink or lay it on top of the glass.

1. Using a vegetable peeler or mandolin, slice thin strips of cucumber lengthwise.
2. Even out the ends of the strips, and cut down to the desired size.
3. Fold in an "S" shape (there can be more than one fold) and secure with a toothpick or skewer.
4. Drop in the drink (optionally adding a mint sprig).

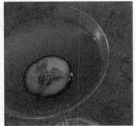 

Cucumber "Horse's Neck"

You will recall the classic citrus garnish called the *horse's neck* discussed in chapter 1, where a strip of citrus is curled on the inside of the glass.

You can accomplish the same with a strip of cucumber.

1. Using a vegetable peeler or mandolin, slice thin strips of cucumber lengthwise.
2. Even out the ends of the strips.
3. Place a strip inside the glass in a spiral shape with one end protruding above the rim.
4. Use a bar spoon to hold the piece in place, and pour the drink in the glass.

Twists

1. Place a cucumber on a cutting board.
2. Cut off and discard the ends.
3. Cut the cucumber in thin slices.
4. Cut a slit in each slice from center to edge.
5. Twist the ends in opposite directions to create a twist.
6. Drop in drink.

Variation: Stack 2 or 3 slices before cutting and twist them together.

Rose

Here's an elegant way to turn a cucumber into an attractive garnish.

It involves rolling thin slices of cucumber to create the illusion of a rose.

1. Cut 5 very thin slices of cucumber using a knife or mandolin.
2. Place slices on top of each over with a half-slice offset.
3. Curl in the top slice tightly and start rolling.
4. Roll all the way to the end, keeping the slices tight.
5. Holding the assembly tightly, trim off the lower portion.
6. Secure with a cocktail stick.
7. Place the stick across the rim of the glass.
8. Spread out the "petals" a little.
9. Sprinkle with spice if desired.

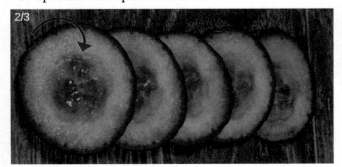

Pinwheel

This garnish is in the same spirit as the previous one (rolling cucumber slices to create a flowery look), but this time we're using a long rectangular slice and cutting diagonal notches, which will then spread out when rolled. You can do this with a zucchini or yellow summer squash as well.

1. Using a vegetable peeler or mandolin, cut slices from a cucumber lengthwise.
2. Make diagonal cuts ⅛" apart along one side of the slice.
3. Roll the slice tightly.
4. Secure with a toothpick and trim it.
5. Make a diagonal cut through all the layers at the bottom of the rolled slice.
6. Place on rim.

Spiral

Create a spiral similar to that commonly created with citrus peels.

1. Using a vegetable peeler or mandolin, cut a thin long slice from a cucumber lengthwise.
2. Hold the slice between thumbs and index fingers, and twist it on itself to form a spiral.
3. Hold for 10 seconds so that it retains its shape.
4. Place on top of the drink.

Cucumber Bowl

This garnish creates a fluted bowl from the end of the cucumber. The bowl can be placed on the rim of the glass or floated in the drink. You can also fill it with something of a contrasting color for a more intense look.

1. Using a paring knife, make a diagonal cut about 2 inches from the end of the cucumber, cutting to the center.
2. Make another diagonal cut perpendicular to the first one.
3. Repeat similar diagonal cuts all around the cucumber, paying attention to end in the same point you started with. Ensure you cut all the way to center each time otherwise the piece will not detach.
4. Carefully twist the end piece back and forth until it separates from the remainder of the cucumber.
5. Even out imperfections in the cuts if necessary.
6. Cut a vertical notch at the bottom of the "bowl" and slide on the rim or float on the drink.

Triangle Twist

This technique produces a triangle garnish with overlapping sides. It can be perched at the top of the glass or dropped in the drink.

1. Cut a ¼" thick piece out of the edge of a cucumber.
2. Straighten the edges to make a rectangle of 3"x1".
3. Cut a partial slit, parallel to the longer side of the rectangle and a third of the width away from the edge (do not cut all the way to the end).
4. Turn the piece around and repeat a similar cut on the other side (again, do not cut all the way).
5. Bend the two "arms" out, and overlap them to form a triangle.

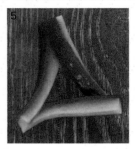

CELERY

Celery is mainly used in a Bloody Marys, and it serves as more than just a decoration. First, it acts as a handy swizzle stick. But it is also meant to be eaten between sips as its astringent qualities help cool the palate from the salty and hot flavors of the drink. Finally, it provides a nice crunch, contrasting with the smooth feel of the liquid.

1. Wash celery stalks well.
2. Trim bottom the stalks off.
3. Optional: cut leaves off (some like the leaves on, some don't).
4. Optionally, slice lengthwise.
5. Drop vertically in drink.

Note that often the Bloody Mary is garnished with more than a celery stick. For instance, in the picture above, we used celery, asparagus, olive and cocktail onion, along with a spicy rim.

CARROTS

Here's a cute "flowery" garnish made from a carrot. In order to create it, you do need a special tool (often called a "carrot curler") that works like a pencil sharpener for carrots.

1. Peel the carrot.
2. Score the carrot along its length using the scraper on the side of the tool (or a channel knife).
3. Turn the carrot through the curler, producing a long curled "shaving" of carrot with indented edges (since we scored the carrot in the previous step).
4. Roll the curl on itself to form a flower.
5. Slide a toothpick sideways to secure.
6. Optionally, place a blackberry on the middle.
7. Push 2 toothpicks from the bottom into the assembly.
8. Hang on the rim with one of the 2 toothpicks on each side of the glass.

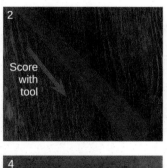
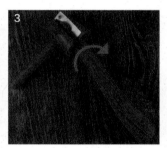

SPICES & CHILES

Spices can be sprinkled on top of a cocktail or on top of another garnish (for instance a slice of apple). The most common ones are cinnamon and nutmeg. You will get better results if you grate them fresh, as opposed to using spices from the store that are already ground.

You can sprinkle them randomly all over the drink, concentrate them in one spot or use a stencil to create a pattern (see chapter 12). A few spices like star anise can be floated on top as you would a flower, and sticks (like cinnamon) can be plunged in the drink.

Finally, feel free to combine several of these techniques as in the examples below.

Chili Flower

Here's an attractive garnish where a red or green chili pepper is turned into a flower.

1. Cut a small chili in half, leaving the stalk intact.
2. Turn the chili 90 degrees, and cut again the same way.
3. Using a very sharp knife, drag the blade through each of the four chili parts to cut each in half. Be careful to not damage other parts.
4. Put in ice water for 30 minutes. The water will enter the chili and push the "petals" outwards.
5. Remove from water and drop in cocktail.

Tips:

- If you don't want to impart too much heat to the cocktail, remove the seeds first
- As an alternative to using a knife, you can just cut the chili in half once then use scissors to cut the petals from it.
- Wear food-grade latex gloves when handling chili peppers. And be careful to not touch your eyes, face or other sensitive areas if your fingers have come in contact with the chili.

Jalapeños

Jalapeños can be sliced and dropped in the drink, acting both as a visual element and a flavoring one. Depending on how spicy you want the drink to be, you may want to remove some or all of the seeds before adding to the drink.

You can also slide a couple of slices on a cocktail stick and drop in the drink or lay across the glass.

Or you could just cut a notch in a slice and attach it to the rim. This way, you add visual appeal and avoid adding heat to the drink.

Crystallized Ginger

Crystallized ginger offers the perfect combination of sweet and spicy zing that makes a great addition to a cocktail. You can buy it at the store, but it is usually expensive. Below is a recipe to make your own. Make sure you buy firm and somewhat tender (but not spongy) ginger.

1. Cut the ginger into the desired shape (either thin slices, strips or cubes).
2. Combine 2 cups of water and 2 cups of sugar in a saucepan.
3. Bring to a boil.
4. Carefully add the ginger, avoiding splattering.
5. Reduce the heat to low, and simmer for 20 minutes, stirring frequently.
6. Remove using a slotted spoon, and place on a wire rack with parchment paper underneath it. Make sure you separate individual pieces so they do not stick to each other.
7. Let dry thoroughly.
8. Place the pieces in a ziplock bag with some sugar, close the bag and shake.
9. Skewer on a cocktail stick and place over the drink. Or store in an airtight container (they will keep for up to 3 months).

Tip: Don't discard the syrup. Use it in place of simple syrup in cocktails. It will bring a little spiciness to your drink.

HERBS

Herbs can sometimes be used to good effect as a garnish. Besides visual appeal, some of the more fragrant ones may contribute some aroma to the cocktail, but usually little in terms of flavor. Of course, you need to make sure the herb is not toxic and is organic and free of pesticides/toxins. Even then, it's still a good idea to give them a rinse and pat them dry before using.

Also, remember to slap the leaves or herb a little to release their fragrance and provide a nice aroma for your guests as they bring the glass to their mouth. But be careful not to crush or bruise it. A quick firm slap between your hands is all it takes to activate the essential oils without tearing the plant, which would potentially release chlorophyll and impart bitterness.

The most commonly used herbs are mint, rosemary, lemon verbena, sage and lovage. Rosemary usually works well with gin, while thyme and cilantro pair nicely with tequila and lemon verbana with rum.

The most typical form of herb used as garnish is the sprig (which usually means about 3 leaves) gently placed on top in a minimalist style or in a bunch (eg: Julep) often placed in a hole made in crushed ice.

A few leaves (or even just one, for a minimalist look) can be arranged and floated on the surface of the drink.

Another simple way to use herbs is to stand a sprig or branch vertically in the glass or floating on the surface. Rosemary and thyme seem to be particularly well suited for this due to the rigidity of their stem.

Leafy herbs (such as sage) can be cut in a chiffonade (ie sliced in thin strips), and either floated on top, or dispersed in the drink. The latter works best with iced drinks, so that the strips can be pushed down into the drink and the ice cubes will keep them in place. The needle-like leaves of rosemary can also be used.

An herb with a strong stem (such as rosemary or tarragon) can be used as a skewer.

Another option is to use herbs as an extra accent for an existing garnish. For example, a sprig of mint will usually add an extra dimension and a touch of contrast to an otherwise bland garnish. To illustrate this, we placed a sprig of mint through the middle of an apple slice.

FLOWERS

Flowers can be a beautiful addition to a drink. You can use blossoms or even individual petals. Of course, as with herbs, make sure they are edible and not covered with pesticides or other toxic material. Edible flowers are very fragile, so they can't be washed easily, which makes it even more important to buy quality ones. Commonly used flowers include hibiscus, rose, lavender, violets, borage and orchids.

As usual, choose a flower that complements the ingredients in the drink. For instance, gin contains many botanicals including some flowers, so it's a good idea to garnish with the same flower that is present in the gin. Lavender works well with most gins and roses are a good complement to Hendrick's gin.

Floating

The simplest way to use flowers is to float them on top of the drink. Some flowers are light enough to float but for others, there's a risk they may sink. So this technique tends to work better with drinks that have a thicker consistency such as those made with egg whites or cream. If the drink is served on ice, you can build the ice to the top and have the flower rest on the cubes.

Here are a few examples.

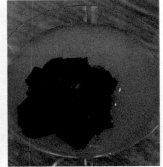

Dispersed in the Drink

For a very unusual and attractive effect, I like dispersing petals (and potentially also herbs) in the drink. The process is pretty simple: carefully remove the petals from the flowers, and place them on top of the drink, then using a straw or knife, gently push them down into the drink. Make sure they are evenly dispersed. This looks even better if you use flowers of different colors. This technique works best for drinks served with ice as the ice will keep the flowers in place, and prevent them from floating to the surface or sinking to the bottom.

Ice Cubes

For a stunning effect, try freezing flowers in ice cubes.

1. Fill an ice cube tray halfway with water.
2. Add flowers or petals. You can use flowers of different colors for variety and even put two different types in one cube.
3. Freeze until the flowers are held in the ice.
4. Fill the rest of the cube tray with cool water.
5. Freeze and unmold the cube when needed.

Rims

Mixing flowers with sugar is an interesting way to flavor the sugar. You typically let the flowers sit in the sugar for a week or so, then pass the mixture through a sieve, and remove the flowers. The resulting sugar can then be used in syrups or muddled in drinks.

You can use this flower-sugar as a rimming ingredient. Place the flowers in sugar for 3 days, then blitz in a food processor. Use the resulting mixture on your rim (see chapter 7 for more information on rims).

On the Rim

Flowers can act as a lovely garnish when attached to the rim of the glass. But attaching them on their own is tricky. So it is usually best to attach them to another garnish as in the example below.

Crystallized Flower Petals

Flower petals can be crystallized for a beautiful effect. Again, make sure you use only edible flowers. Usually only the petals are crystallized, not the entire flower. So carefully pull the petals off the flower first.

1. Preheat oven to 200ºF.
2. Beat 1 egg white with 1 teaspoon of water until frothy and place in a bowl.
3. Fill a glass bowl with water and ¼ teaspoon of salt.
4. Fill another glass bowl with ice water.
5. Set paper towels on the counter.
6. Place the petals in the salted water for 3 minutes.
7. Move the petals to the ice water bowl, and let sit for 3 minutes (they will become firm).
8. Remove the petals from the ice water and place them on paper towels to dry.
9. Pick up the petals one at a time with tweezers, and brush the egg white on both sides (using a small pastry brush).
10. Place the petals on a plate, and sprinkle them with powdered sugar.
11. Place on a baking sheet lined with parchment paper.
12. Place the sheet in the oven, but keep the door open slightly.
13. Dry for about 45 minutes (or until brittle),
14. Place over drink or store in an airtight container (they will keep for up to a year)

Coffee

Coffee beans can make a nice addition to a coffee-based cocktail. Simply float a few beans on top of the drink.

BACON

Bacon has become a trendy ingredient in cocktails. Spearheaded by PDT in New York with their *Benton's Old-Fashioned*, a number of bars are now incorporating bacon flavors in their drinks. The most common technique is fat-washing: liquid fat is mixed with spirit and left to set in the freezer overnight, then the solid fat is scooped out and strained, which results in a spirit imbued with the fat's flavors, as well as an improved mouth feel.

For these drinks, the obvious garnish is a piece of bacon. It can be laid on top of the glass or placed vertically in the drink. A third alternative is to cut a notch through the bacon strip and hang on the glass (half in, half out).

Instead of simply frying the bacon as usual, a good variation is to caramelized it first. This allows you to combine most people's two main food groups (fat and sugar) in one convenient package. Here's how:

1. Preheat oven to 325°F.
2. Toss 6 bacon slices with 2 tablespoons of brown sugar in a bowl until coated.
3. Place a rack over an aluminum-foil-lined baking sheet (to catch the drippings).
4. Lay the bacon on the rack and place in the oven.
5. Bake until crisp (about 30 minutes).
6. Allow to cool fully.
7. Cut to appropriate size.

1. Preheat oven to 400°F.
2. Wrap bacon around a wooden skewer to form a spiral.
3. Place in the oven on a parchment-lined baking sheet.
4. Bake for 10 minutes, turn over and bake for a further 5 minutes.
5. Remove from the oven and place on paper towels to absorb excess oil.
6. Once cooled, remove from the skewer.
7. Place vertically in the drink.

Bacon Spiral

This variation involves baking the bacon in a spiral shape, which you can then place in the drink vertically and use as a swizzle stick. This works best with a thick cut of bacon.

JERKY

Similar to the bacon trend, several bars have started serving jerky with their drinks. Of note, *Comme Ca* in LA offers a strip of beef jerky in one of their drinks named "The Butcher". *PDT* in New York garnishes their "North by Northwest" cocktail with salmon jerky and *Napa Valley Grille* serves a beef swizzle stick in one of their Bloody Marys.

MEAL ON A GLASS

We conclude this chapter on savory garnishes with a discussion on a disturbing trend in the US whereby food is piled and stacked high above a drink. The most common cocktail to be garnished this way is the Bloody Mary, but sometimes it is a punch of sorts (usually labeled "brunch punch"). Though I do not condone this practice, I felt I had to include a section about it in this book for the sake of completeness.

It started fairly innocently with the addition of a few shrimp, cherry tomatoes, or other small items on a skewer to provide the guest with a little food with their Bloody Mary (usually as part of a brunch). But over the years, it has degenerated into a veritable arms race, where bars and restaurants try to outdo each other in both the amount of piled food and its unhealthiness...

Now, we find "garnishes" that are gargantuan feasts (including burgers, pierogies, fried chicken, brownies and pizzas) which would make even Shrek think twice about ordering. Definitely a feat in outrageousness and defiance of gravity, but certainly not in gastronomy, and I suspect the trend was instigated by the American Society of Heart Surgeons!

Here are a few examples of such abominations.

- *Storefront Company* in Chicago serves a punch topped with kumquat and duck three ways (confit, proscuitto and heart).
- *Sobelman's Pub* and Grill in Milwaukee created the "Chicken fried bloody beast", which includes as its center-piece an entire fried chicken accompanied by (among other delights) cheese, sausage, shrimp and skewers of bacon-wrapped jalapeño cheeseballs!
- *Score on Davie* in Vancouver offers a Bloody Caesar (a Canadian Bloody Mary) with a full roasted chicken, a burger, a slider, chicken wings, onion rings, pulled pork mac and cheese, a hot dog and a brownie. They state that it's intended for two people. I know it's tempting, but don't be greedy and try to eat it all by yourself...
- Not to be outdone, *O'Davey's Pub* in Wisconsin created the "Wisconsinite delight", which includes dill cheese curds, a venison stick, beer salami, corn on the cob, roasted asparagus, BBQ rib, prime rib, potatoes and mushrooms, a triple-decker fish sandwich, a bacon-wrapped jalapeño pepper, a bison-and-bacon cheeseburger, chicken wings, bacon, coleslaw and potato salad, a ham roll-up, and whipped mozzarella cheese.

- Finally, comedian Randy Liedtke came up (presumably as a joke but it's really no worse then the others) with a Bloody Mary monstrosity garnished with a whole pepperoni pizza, a footlong sub, fried chicken, two double cheeseburgers, onion rings, fries, and garlic bread and another Bloody Mary.

Inspired by these delicacies, I could not resist the temptation to design my own rendition of these culinary delights. Mine includes a pepperoni pizza, a roast chicken, a triple-cheese burger, a meatball sub, french fries and a stack of donuts, all precariously perched on a small glass of bloody mary.

Enjoy... if you can eat it all, it's on the house...

Chapter 7 – Rims

A simple and common way to add both flair and flavor to a drink is to rim the glass. This means securing a substance (usually salt or sugar, but there are many other options as will be described below) to the top of the glass.

This technique is seen in all levels of bars, but unfortunately, it is often done incorrectly, with less than satisfactory results. The most common mistake is allowing some rimming material to adhere to the inside of the glass. This results in the salt or sugar falling into the drink, affecting the flavor balance. A little salt complements and balances the flavor of a sour nicely, but when more than is required falls in the glass, the drink tastes more like a "brine" than a delicious cocktail.

This section will cover two possible rimming options: the edge (sometimes called tip) and the ribbon (sometimes called band). We will discuss both techniques, as well as the various items used to rim the glass and offer special tips for each.

General Techniques

At a high level, rimming a glass involves a "sticking agent" and the "flavoring agent". The role of the sticking agent is to create a bond between the glass and the flavoring agent. Usually citrus juice is used as the sticking agent, but in some applications, honey or agave nectar can be used. The most common flavoring agents are salt and sugar.

The techniques below are similar regardless of the agent used. So I will use the expressions "sticking agent" and "flavoring agent" generically (by the way, these are terms I use in this book, but are not necessarily widely used). When following the steps, replace these terms by the agent you are using.

The general technique for rimming is to apply the sticking agent to the area of the glass where we want the flavoring agent to be. Then apply the flavoring agent to the glass, and shake off the excess. The flavoring agent will remain only on the sticky surface creating the rim effect.

Tips

- Unless you know your guest's preference, I recommend not rimming the entire edge of the glass. I usually leave at least a quarter and sometimes half of the glass unrimmed, so that the guest can decide whether or not he/she wants the extra flavor imparted by the rimming ingredient.
- Choose your sticking and flavoring agents to match the drink they are decorating. For instance, use lime as your sticking agent in a lime-based sour (such as a margarita). Or use a citrus reminiscent of a liqueur in the drink. For example, you could use orange juice as your sticking agent in a drink that contains triple-sec. Make sure the flavoring agent complements the drink as well, either using a similar flavor that is already in the drink or a complementary flavor that contrasts well with it.
- Use coarser flavoring agents. For instance, use Kosher salt instead of table salt (more details on that in the agents section).
- It's a good idea to prepare rimmed glasses ahead of time. Not only does it save time during service, it allows the sticking agent to dry and adhere better.

Creating an Edge

In this technique, the flavoring agent is applied to the very top of the glass.

It is the best option for drinks that contain no ice, as the ice can affect the delicate balance of the agent on the tip.

1. Prepare a shallow bowl with ½" of the flavoring agent.
2. Even out the level of the agent by shaking the bowl. You may need to re-level the agent periodically as you use it (potentially even between each glass). Eventually, the sticking agent will cause the flavoring agent to clump together creating an uneven product. At that point, dispose of it and prepare a new batch.
3. You have two options for moistening the glass:
    a. When using a citrus, hold the fruit in one hand and the glass in the other, run the fruit around the glass lightly (or keep the fruit steady and turn the glass) making sure you only touch the very tip of the glass.
    b. Prepare a bowl with sticking agent (if using citrus, use fresh squeezed juice and not prepackaged cordials such as Rose's lime juice) and dip the very tip of the glass in the bowl.
4. Carefully dip the tip of the glass in the flavoring agent. Keep in mind that, with this technique, you only want a little agent on the very tip. It often works better to tip the glass at an angle and do one section at a time, tapping the excess in between. This is particularly crucial if you are not rimming the entire glass.
5. Holding the glass upside down, tap it lightly to dislodge any flavoring agent that has not adhered to the glass.

CREATING A RIBBON

The ribbon appears as a belt or band at the top of the glass. It is the best option for drinks served with ice. Since the agent is only on the outside, it will not be dislodged as you add ice (as would be the case with the edge technique). It's up to you how wide you make the ribbon but it is typically ½" to ¾".

This technique works better with citrus since you can control the moistening width by the size of the citrus wedge. If you want to use this technique with a more syrupy agent such as agave nectar, you may end up with an uneven band. This is not necessarily a bad thing (it gives it a more rustic look). If you want to have a straight band with syrup, you can use food-grade masking tape.

The steps below will assume you are using a citrus.

1. Prepare a shallow bowl with ½" of the flavoring agent.
2. Even out the level of the agent by shaking the bowl. You may need to re-level the agent periodically as you use it (potentially even between each glass). Eventually the sticking agent will cause the flavoring agent to clump together creating an uneven product. At that point, dispose of it and prepare a new batch.
3. Cut a wedge out of a citrus.
4. Cut the wedge in half through the flesh but not the skin, then remove half of the flesh. You are left with a full skin and half the flesh. The reason for this is that it allows us to use the skin as a guide on top of the glass for an even band, while allowing only the outside to be touched by the citrus (ie the flavoring agent will only stick to the outside).

5. For a narrower band, cut off some of the flesh on the inside.
6. Place the citrus piece on the glass (flesh on the outside) and rotate it around the rim. Use the skin to maintain the wedge level, otherwise you will end up with an uneven ribbon.
7. Go all the way around the glass (or partly if leaving an unrimmed area)
8. Hold the glass by the base or stem at a 45 degree angle, roll the glass in the flavoring agent.
9. Tap off the excess.
10. Using a wet paper towel, clean up the glass if any rimming agent accidentally made it on the inside.

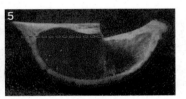

RIMMING AGENTS

Salt

Salt naturally balances sourness and sweetness. Bartenders often use a saline solution to bring balance to their sours, but using a salt rim is another useful way to achieve this.

When using salt, make sure to use a large-flake salt (such as kosher salt or sea salt). Salts can be mixed with spices (especially if the drink itself is spicy). Again, it is best to use chili flakes rather than fine powders. Finally, you can use celery salt (as long as celery goes with the flavors of the drink).

Sugar

When using sugar as your flavoring agent, choose a sugar with larger crystal. Steer clear of very fine sugars and powdered sugars. Personally, I like using turbinado or demerara sugar. Colored sugars can be used for a more intense look. In this example, a red rim is paired with a caramelized blood orange slice for a dramatic look.

Nuts

If your drink contains a strong nut-flavored ingredient (such as Frangelico or Amaretto) you may want to consider creating a rim of the same nut. I occasionally use nut rims when I want to introduce a specific nut flavor in a cocktail, but the nut in question is too mild to impart significant flavor to the drink itself.

You can either grind the nuts in a spice grinder or give them a rough chop depending on the texture you want to create. For the latter, since the pieces are heavier, a sticking agent heavier than citrus juice will be required. Consider using honey, agave nectar or caramel. Make sure these are thick and not watery, otherwise they will drip down the side of the glass over time and look messy.

Coconut

Coconut flakes can also be used with great success on a rim. It is particularly important here to ensure that the flakes are only on the outside of the glass as they tend to fall off and you don't want to have floating specs of coconut in the drink.

Chocolate

A chocolate rim is the natural partner for any chocolate-based drink like chocolate martinis or chocolate-flavored creamy after-dinner cocktails.

You have two main options:

- Powders. Using cocoa powder provide an elegant decoration for the glass. The edge technique lends itself better to powders, so that's usually what I use.

Some people may find cocoa powder too bitter, so you may want to use a hot-chocolate powder instead. It will look visually similar but will have a little sweetness to it.

- Sprinkles/shavings. For sprinkles, I prefer the edge method using melted chocolate as my sticking agent.

Once you've dipped the tip of the glass in melted chocolate, dip it in a bowl of chocolate sprinkles or shavings. Make sure the melted chocolate is liquid but not overly hot, otherwise the sprinkles will melt when applied. Place the glasses in the refrigerator or freezer to allow the edge to set and prevent remelting if the room temperature is high. You may also want to consider tempering the chocolate to allow it to stay stable at room temperature (see chapter 10 for details on tempering).

Note that you can also use cocoa nibs, but they may be too bitter for some people.

Powdered Liqueur

For an unusual variation, consider drying up some liqueur and using it to create a rim.

1. Pour a high-sugar, strongly flavored liqueur like Chartreuse or Campari in a shallow dish.
2. Let dry completely (it may take several days depending on the moisture in the environment). At this point, you will have a crystallized mass.
3. Put in mortar and use pestle to grind to a powder.
4. Use the powder as a flavoring agent.

Other ideas

Here are a few random ideas to inspire you. This is by no means an exhaustive list. Use your creativity but remember, as always, to match the rim flavor to the drink's flavor.

- Spices: add coarsely ground spices to your salt for a spicy kick.
- Zest: using a microplane, zest a citrus, use a paper towel to absorb moisture, and let dry. Then coarsely chop and add to your rimming agent.
- Black sea salt: for a different look on a salted rim, try black sea salt.
- Cookie: For sweet after-dinner drinks, cookies can be used. Crush the cookies to the desired size based on the texture you are looking for, and use agave nectar or thick caramel to attach them to the glass
- Gingersnap: for a holiday-inspired cocktail, you may want to consider using gingersnaps.
- Graham Crackers
- Crushed hard candies

- Mini-marshmallows
- Coconut flakes
- Colored sugar sprinkles
- Edible gold flakes
- Dried or fresh herbs
- Edible flowers (see chapter 6 for details).

Corral Frosting

Corral frosting is a technique popularized by Japanese bartender Kazuo Uyeda. It is meant to evoke a corral reef. This is a very cool and unusual effect that is sure to intrigue your guests. This technique works better with a vertical-edged glass rather than a conical one.

1. Place salt in a bowl. The depth of the salt should be the height of the corral effect you want to obtain
2. Place blue curacao in another bowl. The height of the curacao should be half that of the salt.
3. Hold the glass upside down and plunge it in the curacao bowl.
4. Without turning it over, dip the glass straight down into the salt.
5. Lift the glass up and turn it right side up.
6. Clean out salt from the inside of the glass. Depending on whether or not you want the guest to get a salty flavor, you may also want to clear out the immediate edge of the glass. But be careful not to damage the corral design in the process.

The steps above will result in a blue corral. But you can create other colors by using different liqueurs/cordials (for instance, use Midori for green, grenadine for red/purple, etc...)

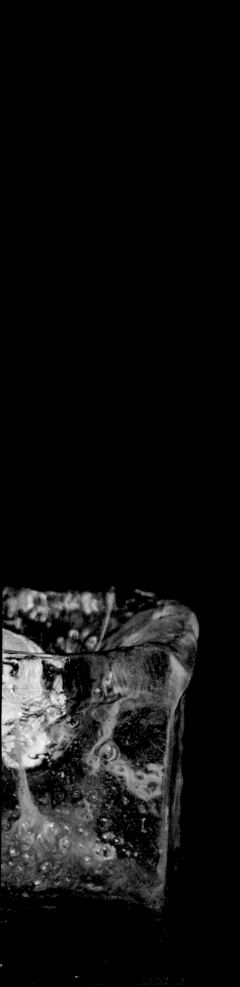

Chapter 8 – Fire and Ice

This chapter will cover two opposite elements, fire and ice and their use as cocktail garnishes.

On the fire side, we will cover the blue blazer, flaming a twist and floating flames.

And for the ice side, we will discuss various techniques to create more attractive ice for your drinks (clear, colored, garnished,...), as well as a few cool tricks such as the ice bowl and serving a cocktail in an ice sphere.

FIRE

Though seen as a gimmick by some, fire can add flair to your cocktail. Using a flame to enhance flavor ("flamber" as the French call it) is not a new concept. This technique has been used in dishes such as steak Diane, Bananas Fosters, Crêpe Suzette and the traditional Christmas pudding. As with most cocktail history, it is not clear when flaming was introduced to mixology. The first documented use of fire in cocktails appears in 1862 in Jerry Thomas' classic bartender manual "How to Mix Drinks: Or, The Bon-vivant's Companion". The recipe was named Blue Blazer and described how to create a "blazing stream of liquid fire" by pouring lit-up scotch between two metal mugs (see next page for details).

Today, very few bars actually produce blue blazers. What you are more likely to find are either a constant flame burning on top of the drink (typical in tiki drinks), or most commonly a brief flash of fire created by expressing the oils of a citrus through a flame.

High-proof liquor needs to be used or it will not light up as expected. The flaming effect has both visual benefits, adding drama and flair to the cocktail, as well as potentially enhancing the flavor of the drink.

Safety Notes

It goes without saying that using fire and alcohol is a potentially risky activity. Safety guidelines need to be followed to protect not only the guest but also the bartender (and the bar itself).

1. The flame should be extinguished before the drink is consumed.
2. Even after the flame is extinguished, the liquid and/or the container may still be hot. Make sure you wait for it to properly cool before serving or consuming.
3. Use a container that can handle the heat. The ceramic of tiki mugs is usually heat-resistant, but a flimsy glass may not be (use tempered glass).
4. Keep the area clear of other bottles. For instance, a half-empty bottle may emanate fumes which could potentially ignite and cause the bottle to explode.
5. Make sure alcohol does not spill outside the container, otherwise the flame may follow the spill and light up the bar or – God forbid – a guest.
6. Have a fire extinguisher or wet towel handy in case things get out of hand.

7. Finally, just use common sense and stay safe. The author and publisher of this book accept no responsibility for injuries or destruction of property resulting from attempting any of the techniques below.

If you need convincing about the dangers of fire and alcohol, search for "Funny Flaming Shot Fail Compilation" on YouTube.

Flaming Shots

The easiest way to use fire as a garnish is to simply light shots. Though you can light the shot glass directly, it may take longer to heat up. Here's a faster procedure:

1. Fill a shot glass almost to the top.
2. Fill a spoon with the same spirit.
3. Light the contents of the spoon with a lighter.
4. Pour into the shot glass.
5. Blow the shot out before serving to your guest.

Tips

- This works better with high-proof spirits since they can be lit at room temperature. Weaker spirits need to be heated first.
- Don't underfill the glass or it may crack.
- Don't fill the glass to the brim or it may spill and start a fire.

Blue Blazer

As discussed in the introduction to this section, the blue blazer is an impressive, albeit risky, technique developed by Jerry Thomas in the 19th century. It involves pouring flaming streams of scotch back and forth between two mugs, before finally adding sugar and lemon, thereby creating a toddy.

The mugs are a bit of a specialized item: made of metal with handles and flared rims (to facilitate pouring).

Ingredients (makes 4 cocktails)
- 5 ounces cask-strength scotch whisky
- ½ cup boiling water
- 4 strips of lemon peel (1" wide)
- 4 teaspoons raw sugar

Steps
1. Set up 4 small coffee cups, each with a teaspoon of sugar and a strip of lemon peel.
2. For safety reason, make sure all other bottles of alcohol (and any other flammable items) are kept at a safe distance.
3. It is also helpful to have damp clothes laid down to catch the inevitable spills.
4. Dim the lights so that the effects of the burning blue flame are more visible.
5. Pour the boiling water into one of the metal mixing mugs.
6. Add the whisky to the same mug.
7. Light the water/whisky mixture with a long match or long lighter (like those used for a grill).
8. Pour about three quarters of the flaming mixture into the other cup.
9. Pour back and forth 4-5 times, with increasing distance between the cups each time, as much as you feel comfortable doing without spilling everything and burning the whole place down! It takes practice (I recommend practicing with just water initially until you get it right). If this is done well, it will give the impression of a continuous stream of liquid fire.
10. Pour into the prepared coffee cups (it will still be flaming at this point).
11. Extinguish the fire in each cup (and whatever else you set on fire during the process!) using the bottom of one of the mugs.
12. Give a quick stir so that the sugar dissolves.
13. Serve.
14. Breath a sigh of relief that your place is not burning down (or call 911 if it is).

Flamed Citrus Twist

This is the most popular flaming trick. It was allegedly designed by Pepe Ruiz for a special cocktail made for Dean Martin. Dale Degroff also had a part in popularizing this trick in the 80s. Since citrus skin contains some flammable oils, by squeezing those oils out through a flame, one can produce a brief burst of fire. Orange is the most commonly used citrus for this (but you can also use lemons).

Whenever a recipe calls for a citrus twist, you can use this variation. But the flavor differences between a regular citrus twist and its flamed counterpart are minimal in my opinion. So, this is done more for visual and theatrical reasons rather than culinary ones.

1. Select a citrus fruit that is very fresh as it will have more oil in the skin. I also prefer organic fruit as I'd rather not be squirting pesticide residue into my drink...

2. Cut a swath (or a circle) out of a citrus. Slice it thick to make it easier to squeeze.

3. Light a match, lighter or propane torch.

4. Optional. Warm the citrus briefly with the flame. I marked this step as optional because, even though a lot of bartenders do this, there's debate as to whether it makes a lot of difference to the results.

5. Hold the match or torch in one hand (a few inches above the drink) and the citrus swath (skin facing the flame and a few inches from it) in the other hand between thumb and index finger, keeping the flame between the citrus and the top of the drink.

6. Sharply squeeze the top and bottom of the swath to express the oils, which will pass through the flame and land on top of the drink's surface (like a normal twist) and produce a flash of fire in the process.

7. Wipe the rim of the glass with the citrus peel as you would with a normal twist.

8. Drop in the drink (or not, see note in chapter 1).

Floating Flame

Another common way to add a flame to a drink is to float a vessel of sorts on the drink, and have a flame burn in it. A hollowed-out lemon or lime is often used as the container, though a small fire-resistant dish is sometimes used instead. If you use a citrus, your guest will also benefit from the nice smoked citrus aroma.

The vessel is typically filled with high-proof rum and set alight. This creates a blueish flame that is sometimes hard to see depending on the ambient light. A lot of people prefer to use pure lemon extract instead of rum (note that imitation extract will not work).

You can also use a crouton or a sugar cube doused in high-proof rum or pure lemon extract, and set it alight. These act as a "wick" creating a better, taller flame. They also weight down the vessel a little making it more stable and less prone to tipping. Of the two options, I personally prefer the sugar cube as I find the resulting charred crouton unappealing.

While the cocktail is burning, you can sprinkle spices (such as cinnamon) from a shaker on top of the flame in order to toast them and release their aroma, and of course provide a nice show for your guests.

Some bartenders like to put bitters or some spirit in an atomizer bottle and spray it into the flame while sprinkling the spices to create extra drama.

Absinthe Bohemian Ritual

Absinthe drinking is full of rituals. A Czec/Bohemian version involves dousing a sugar Cube with absinthe, setting it on an absinthe spoon over the drink and lighting it on fire. As the fire burns, the sugar caramelizes and drips into the glass imparting an interesting caramel flavor to the drink.

ICE

In this section, we will discuss the use of ice as a decorative item. Ice is, of course, an essential ingredient in cocktail making, but I will not discuss here its normal use (in shaking and stirring drinks). We will focus on the visual aspects of ice. In particular, we will discuss how to create ice which is more attractive than the ice typically made by your fridge. We will also see how we can use ice in innovative ways such a creating an ice bowl, encasing items in ice and serving a cocktail in an ice sphere.

Clear Ice

When a drink is served with ice, the attractiveness of the ice plays a vital role in the visual appeal of the drink. In particular, clear ice yields a better-looking drink than the typical cloudy grayish ice we're used to. This cloudiness is caused by minerals and gases trapped in the ice as it freezes. The trick to making clear ice is to slow the freezing process, so that these minerals and gases are able to rise to the surface.

Professionals invest in industrial machines that freeze the ice slowly, in layers from the bottom (which pushes gases out in the process), but these are very expensive and out of reach of the home enthusiast. Also, they produce giant blocks of ice (300 lb), which are impractical unless you're running a busy bar.

So, what options do we have to create clear ice at home? There are a lot of posts online suggesting to boil the water first before freezing, but I have not seen this technique make much difference to the end product. What does help to some extent is using distilled water as it will at least be free of impurities.

There are some smaller and simpler versions of the big professional ice machines. These cost a couple hundred dollars and are not quite as good as the industrial equipment, but they do produce decent results and in batches more appropriate for the home setting.

Another option is to freeze the water at a relatively high temperature, but still below freezing (like 30°F). This is difficult to achieve in a normal freezer, which is usually a lot colder. Also, this temperature is too high for other items in your freezer, so you need to have a dedicated freezer for this purpose. Some have achieved success by placing their ice-tray in a mini-fridge's freezer compartment set on the warmest setting, but you need patience as it will take several days for the ice to be fully frozen. The other advantage of having a dedicated freezer is that the ice won't pick up odors from the other items in the fridge. Nothing worse than a perfectly balanced drink ruined by ice that tastes like pepperoni pizza...

Large Ice Cube

When serving a cocktail on ice, you have the option of placing one large ice cube in the drink instead of several small ones. Besides the more dramatic effect it creates, it also has the advantage of diluting the drink slower (since less surface is exposed to the liquid). There are ice cube trays with larger holes designed for this purpose. The same technique of slow freezing applies here if you want clear cubes.

Ice Spear

Spears create a more dramatic effect in a glass than cubes. You can create them by making a special mold from a standard ice cube tray: carefully cut out the partitions in the tray to make a long rectangle of the desired size. Then freeze as described earlier.

Ice Sphere

A sphere is another dramatic variation on the ice cube that adds to the presentation of your drink.

Like the other larger cubes discussed above, the large ice sphere also helps reducing the speed of dilution compared to smaller cubes.

There are two ways to accomplish this:

Carving
1. Take a large ice cube.
2. Using a serrated knife, cut the corners from the cube.
3. Holding the cube with a towel (to avoid melting it), chip away bits of ice with the serrated knife to create a rounder shape.
4. Rinse the ball under the tap to even out the surface.
5. Dry and place in freezer.

Mold
1. Buy a spherical ice mold. These usually come in two parts that fit together.
2. Fill the bottom part (white) to the fill line.
3. Place the top part over the bottom one.
4. Place in the freezer.
5. When frozen solid, unmold and serve.

The carving method is more labor intensive and creates a less perfect sphere, but if you're starting with a block of clear ice, your sphere will be clear too. The mold method on the other hand is definitely easier, but will usually result in a more cloudy sphere (unless you use the slow freezing method described earlier).

Frozen Grapes

As an alternative to using ice cubes, freeze grapes and use them as ice cubes. This has the advantage of keeping the drink cold without diluting it or adding any flavor.

In this example, I used three frozen grapes to keep a champagne cocktail cool.

Colored Ice Cubes

A cool way to jazz up your ice cubes is to color them. You can use commercial food coloring but I prefer to use natural products. Here's a list of natural ingredients you can use to create a given color. These are not very flavorful so they will not significantly alter the flavor of the drink as they melt.

- Red: beet juice or pomegranate juice.
- Orange: carrot juice or orange beet juice.
- Yellow: turmeric or yellow beet juice.
- Blue: blueberry.
- Purple: blackberry.
- Black: squid ink.
- Green: combine blue and yellow.

To create the colored ice cube, mix the food coloring and water, then pour in your ice-tray and freeze. Pastel colors tend to look better than garish ones. So go easy on the coloring agent.

For an interesting variation, you can create multiple layers of different colors by freezing one layers fully, then adding another color and freezing it.

Cocktail Ice Cubes

Another idea is to use some of the ingredients from the cocktail to make ice cubes. As they melt, they release flavors into the drink, rather than diluting it. High alcohol content items will not freeze, so limit this technique to juices and low ABV liqueurs.

Garnished Ice Cubes

For an impressive look, consider embedding items in your ice cubes. Here are a few examples to get you started, but this is not an exhaustive list:

- Maraschino cherries
- Berries (raspberries, blueberries,...)
- Pieces of a citrus wheel or wedge
- Pieces of fresh fruit
- Melon balls
- Candied fruit
- Mint leaves (or other herbs)
- Edible flowers

Here are the general steps to create garnished cubes:

1. Start with plain water or colored water (as described earlier). If using color, err on the side of less color, otherwise you may not be able to see the item in the ice cube.
2. Fill an ice-tray a third of the way with water.
3. Put the tray in the freezer and partially freeze (it should be slushy, not frozen solid)
4. Place the item (fruit, flower, leaf,...) in position in the partially frozen ice. You can also combine two different items in the same cube as long as they are small enough and do not look overcrowded.
5. Put the tray back in the freezer until the water is fully frozen (the item should now be embedded in the ice, which will prevent it from floating up in the next step).
6. Add ice water to the tray until 80% full.
7. Finish freezing.
8. Unmold and serve as you would normal ice cubes.

As described in the clear ice section, it is best to freeze the cubes slowly otherwise you may end up with a cloudy appearance which will detract from the beauty of the garnish and potentially obscure the content.

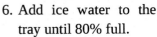

Punch Ice Ring

When making punch for a cocktail party, the challenge is to keep the liquid cold for the duration of the party. A common way to achieve that is to make a big ring of ice and float it in the punch. In its simplest form, the ring is made of water, but it is better to make it of ingredients that are in the punch, so that as it melts it reinforces the flavors instead of diluting them.

We can make this ring more attractive by embedding items in it, similar to the method described earlier with ice cubes. The list of options is similar, but it is most common to use fresh fruits reminiscent of the fruit flavors in the punch.

1. Arrange the fruits at the bottom of a ring mold or bundt pan of a size that will fit comfortably in your punch bowl. Use your artistic talent to create interesting patterns such as alternating fruits with potentially overlapping layers and interspersed herbs and leaves. Remember that this arrangement will be visible for hours during the cocktail party, so take time to create something attractive.
2. Add water (and juices to taste) to barely cover the fruits (they should not float)
3. Freeze slowly until solid.
4. Fill the rest of the mold with more water (or juice).
5. Freeze slowly until solid.
6. Take out of the freezer 5 minutes before serving to facilitate unmolding.
7. Unmold and carefully place in the punch bowl (fruit-side up).
8. Enjoy the rest of the cocktail party.

Ice Bowl

For an unusual ice garnish, create a small bowl made of ice and place it on top of the drink. The bowl can then be filled with items such as small berries, pomegranate seeds and perhaps a sprig of mint. You can also use caviar spheres (see the spherification technique in chapter 11 for details on how to create these).

1. Line a small glass curved-bottom bowl with plastic wrap.
2. Put some crushed ice at the bottom of the bowl.
3. Add some ice water.
4. Line the bottom of another bowl of the same size with plastic wrap and place it in the first bowl, which pushes the ice and water down and up the sides. Depending on the weight of your bowl, you may need to add weight to keep the bowl down.
5. Place the bowls in the freezer until frozen solid.
6. Remove from the freezer and let sit for a minute.
7. Gently twist the top bowl off.
8. Carefully use the plastic wrap to pull the ice bowl free of its container, and peel off the plastic.
9. Place the ice bowl back in the freezer.
10. When ready to serve, remove the ice bowl from the freezer and place on the drink.
11. Add berries and herbs as desired.

Ice Sphere Cocktail

Here's a cool twist on using ice. Instead of adding ice to your drink, how about serving your drink in ice. Sounds crazy? Maybe... Here's how it works.

The cocktail is served in a hollow ice sphere and placed in the glass. It is served with a small mallet for the guest to crack the sphere into the glass.

Professionals working at high-end bars will typically use a gadget called a cold immersion circulator. These work really well for this purpose, but they are expensive and out of reach of the home enthusiast. You can create the same effect with the round ice mold we introduced earlier in this chapter.

You will also need a large syringe with a 2" (or more) needle. Make sure the syringe and needle are used for this purpose only.

1. Fill the round ice mold to the fill line with distilled water (see instructions earlier).
2. Close the mold and place in very cold freezer (as cold as you can get it) and in the coldest part of the freezer, ensuring air can circulate around it.
3. Leave in the freezer for 2-3 hours, flipping upside down halfway through. The exact time will vary based on your freezer. Shoot for an ice wall of ¼". You will need to experiment to find what works for you.
4. Remove the mold from the freezer.
5. There may be half frozen water on top. If so, remove this excess.
6. The sphere will be frozen on the outside but liquid in the center which allows us to remove the liquid through the top hole.
7. Insert the syringe needle into the hole at the top of the sphere and remove all unfrozen water.
8. Set the ice sphere aside in the freezer until ready to use.
9. Make a cocktail of your choice, ensuring it is really cold.
10. Pull the cocktail into the syringe.
11. Slowly fill the prepared sphere with the cocktail (you may need to recreate a hole if it had closed up).
12. When ready to serve, unmold the sphere.
13. Carefully lower the sphere into a rocks glass.
14. Serve with a small hammer or mallet and instruct the guest to break it or break it for them (hopefully without breaking the glass...)

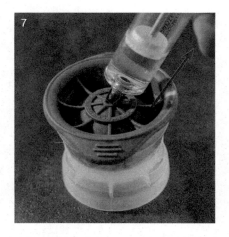

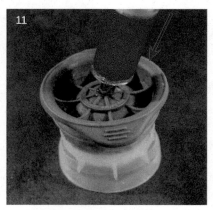

Chapter 9 – Sugar Work

Sugar is an essential component of most cocktails, introduced by syrups, juices or liqueurs. In this chapter, we cover how to use sugar to create garnishes too.

You will learn how to caramelize sugar and use it to create decorations such as lattices, cages and corkscrews.

We will also cover how to *brûler* the top of a cocktail, caramelize a glass and even make spun sugar and cotton candy.

Finally, we will discuss how to candy and caramelize fruits and use them as garnishes.

INTRODUCTION

Sugar (and in particular caramel) offers an infinite number of possibilities for garnishes since it can be shaped, molded, twisted, spun, pulled and even blown into almost any shape. This chapter will draw inspiration from the pastry world where these techniques have been perfected and adapt them to the cocktail garnish.

Temperature is a key element of good sugar work, and it is important to follow the temperatures specified in the recipes. So, it is important to use a good sugar thermometer.

A Word of Caution

Caramel gets very hot and will burn the skin if it comes in contact with it (it is over 100°F hotter than boiling water!). So, exercise caution when handling it. Wearing latex gloves is a good idea as it will protect your hands to some extent. Also keep children and pets away when you are working with melted sugar.

If you do get it on your skin, run cold water over it immediately for at least 5 minutes.

Storage

It is best to use your sugar creations as soon as possible, as the caramel will absorb ambient moisture and start losing its shape and get sticky. If you need to keep them longer, spray them with edible lacquer and/or keep them in an air tight container with food-grade moisture-absorbing packets.

CARAMELIZING SUGAR

A number of the garnishes described in this chapter rely on caramelized sugar. Sugar starts to caramelize and turn golden brown when it reaches 320°F. Here is the recipe to create that caramel.

1. Mix 1 pound of sugar and ½ cup of water in a stainless steel saucepan.
2. Prepare a bowl of water large enough to hold the saucepan.
3. Place the pan on low heat until the sugar is dissolved.
4. Increase the heat and bring to a boil stirring constantly.
5. Add 3 ½ ounces of light corn syrup, stir and bring back to a boil.
6. Continue cooking, washing down the sides with a pastry brush dipped in water. Insert a thermometer and do not stir anymore.

7. When the liquid starts turning amber, we are pretty close to the desired point (about 315°F).
8. As the liquid begins to turn slightly golden brown, remove the pan from the heat, and, still holding it, dip the bottom of the pan in the bowl of water to stop the cooking process.
9. Once the bubbling has stopped, remove the pan from the water, place on a trivet and let cool.
10. Use the caramel as directed in the instructions.

CARAMEL LATTICE

This garnish takes the shape of a flat mesh of caramel, which you can place over the glass. You can create any pattern you like, whether regular or random, but make sure it is not too tight. You should be able to see through the lattice and be able to place a straw through it (if your drink requires one).

1. Lay out a silicon mat and apply a thin coat of vegetable oil.
2. Prepare caramelized sugar as described above.
3. Let it cool until it is thick enough to be spooned and drizzle without running.
4. Take a spoonful of syrup and drip it onto the silicon mat, randomly criss-crossing the drips to create a

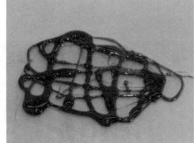

pattern. Cover an area a little bigger than the top of the glass you are planning to use the garnish on. You can make your drizzles thin or thick. I like to mix thicker ones for sturdiness with thinner ones for elegance.

5. Allow to cool until hard.
6. Gently peel the garnish from the mat.
7. Place on top of the glass.

Variations

Instead of placing the garnish over the top of the glass, you can dunk it in, but make sure most of it is still sticking out.

As an alternative to spooning a lattice, you can spoon a circle of about the diameter of your glass's rim and balance the caramel garnish on it.

CARAMEL BASKET

This is a similar idea to the lattice, but this time the garnish is shaped like a half-sphere (instead of being flat), by drizzling the caramel on the back of a ladle. This results in a basket which can be placed it over a drink. You can also place small items (such as berries, nuts, pieces of citrus peel, flowers, etc.) in the basket to add interest.

These garnishes are fragile and break easily. So, be careful when handling them and don't be discouraged if you break a few.

1. Oil the back of a metal ladle with vegetable oil.
2. Prepare a caramelized sugar as described earlier.
3. Let it cool until it is thick enough to be spooned and drizzled without running.
4. Hold the ladle upside down away from your body, over a silicon mat (or similar) to catch drip.
5. With the other hand, spoon some caramel and drizzle it over the ladle. You can do perpendicular lines, but it's easier to just drizzle in a more random fashion. However, make sure each line  connects to the others, otherwise the basket won't hold together. Also, keep the amount of drizzling light enough to be able to see through the pattern.
6. Let the caramel cool and harden (it can take from 10 seconds to a minute).
7. Take a hold of the caramel basket and twist gently to remove from the ladle.
8. Place the basket on top of the drink with small piece of fruit or nuts in it (it will need to rest on the edge of the glass or on the ice in the drink). Serve with a straw through it if appropriate for the drink.

Variation

Instead of serving the half-sphere round-side-down, place it round-side-up over the glass forming a cage or dome. Serve with a small plate so the guest can place the decoration on it before drinking.

CARAMEL CORKSCREW

Here's an impressive caramel garnish that is actually fairly easy and safe to make, since the caramel used is cooler and thicker than other garnishes. This time we're winding the caramel into a spiral shape to be placed on top of the glass.

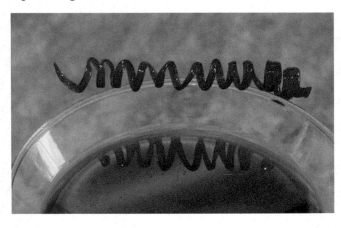

The corkscrew is created by spooning the caramel around a cylinder. A knife sharpening steel is a good tool for that purpose, since it's the right diameter and the grooves prevent sticking. You can also use a dowel or a metal straw (as illustrated here).

1. Oil a sheet of baking paper, where you will place the corkscrews once formed.
2. Lightly spay a sharpening steel with vegetable oil.
3. Prepare caramelized sugar as described earlier.
4. Let the caramel cool longer than you would for the basket or lattice. It needs to be much thicker (thick enough to pull as a thread instead of just flowing).
5. Dip the spoon in the caramel and swirl it until it sticks.
6. Pull a thread of caramel out of the pot (if it runs, let it cool some more).
7. Hold the sharpening steel or metal straw in the other hand horizontally.
8. Quickly work the spoon around the sharpening steel to form a spiral of caramel around it.
9. Let cool until solid.
10. Pull the spiral off the sharpening steel and place on the oiled paper.
11. Carefully trim the ends if necessary.
12. When ready to use, pour the drink and place the corkscrew on the rim of the glass.

Note: these techniques take a bit of practice to master. Do not get discouraged if the first few don't turn out perfect.

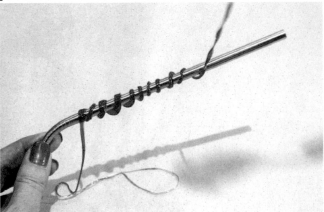

COCKTAIL BRÛLÉ

We're all familiar with *crème brûlée* and its delicious, hard caramelized layer. Why not create the same effect on top of a cocktail.

Prepare a cocktail of your choice (this will work better on a creamy cocktail), and pour in a glass (use tempered glass), then sprinkle a thin layer of sugar over the top of the drink. It's probably best to not cover the entirety of the surface otherwise there won't be a place to drink from.

Using a small propane torch, gently caramelize the sugar. Do not stay too long in one spot; instead, make back and forth motions until the sugar is evenly caramelized (but not burnt).

Let the sugar cool before serving. Also check the temperature of the glass; if you stayed too close to the edge with the flame, the rim may need to cool before serving. Serve with a spoon so your guest can pick up the caramelized layer and eat it.

CARAMEL-DIPPED FRUITS AND NUTS

For an elegant and impressive presentation, consider dipping pieces of fruit or nuts in caramel. For bonus points, you can let the caramel drip and solidify, thereby creating a "tail". You can do this with any fruit or nut you like, but it works better if they have a pointy side (so that the caramel drips down that side more easily).

1. Place baking paper on the floor near the table where you'll be working.
2. Place a ruler on the edge of the table with a big weight on each side.
3. Prepare caramelized sugar as described earlier.
4. Let the syrup cool until very thick but still liquid.
5. Insert a skewer into the fruit or nut. Arrange the skewer so that the pointy end of the dipped item is pointing down. Be careful when using nuts not to push the skewer too far and split the nut.
6. Dip the item in the caramel and lift out.
7. Place the skewer under the ruler. The dipped item should hang over the edge of the table, and the caramel should slowly drip down to make a thin tail. The paper on the floor is there to catch excess drips.
8. Once the caramel has hardened, cut the tail to the desired length using a knife heated in hot water.
9. Using a latex glove on one hand, pick up the caramelized item and remove the skewer with the other hand.
10. Carefully place the item on top of the drink. Alternatively, you can cut a notch in the item (on the opposite side of the tail) using a hot knife, and hang on the rim.

CARAMELIZED GLASS

Another idea is to caramelize part of the glass (usually the rim area, but potentially down the sides). First, a word of warning: only use glassware made with tempered glass for this technique, as a regular glass will not be able to withstand the high heat and will probably shatter.

1. Rim a glass with sugar (see chapter 7 for details).
2. If you want to caramelize more than just the rim, but rub the citrus over the larger area, then sprinkle sugar on it and shake the excess.
3. Using a small propane torch (as used for *crème brûlée*), heat the sugar until it caramelizes and turns golden brown. Do not stay too long in one spot; instead, make back and forth motions until the sugar is evenly caramelized. Heat both inside and outside of the glass to ensure all the sugar is caramelized.

4. Let the sugar harden and the glass cool before pouring and serving the drink.

SPUN SUGAR

Spun sugar is a very impressive but easy way to decorate desserts. It is used a lot in French pastry on top of large cakes like the *St-Honoré* and icecream desserts. We use the same technique here to top a cocktail with wispy strands of sugar.

1. Using a metal cutter, cut off the end of an old metal hand whisk.
2. Place parchment paper on the counter.
3. Place a large glass bowl on top of the paper.
4. Prepare a bowl of water large enough to hold the bottom of the saucepan.
5. Place 20 ounces of sugar and ½ cup of water in a saucepan.
6. Heat the pan over low heat until the mixture starts to boil.

7. Stir in 4 ounces of light corn syrup. Place a thermometer in the liquid and do not stir after this.

8. Increase the heat, and boil until the temperature reaches 265°F.

9. Optionally, add food coloring at this point.

10. Continue boiling until the syrup reaches 310°F.

11. Remove from heat and, still holding the pan, place the bottom of it in the bowl of water.

12. Place the pan on a trivet and let the syrup thicken a little.

13. Dip your cut whisk in the syrup (about ½").

14. Quickly flick the whisk over the glass bowl.

15. Repeat until enough strands of sugar have accumulated over the bowl. It will sort of look like a spider's web.

16. Gather the threads of sugar and place on top of a cocktail.

COTTON CANDY

Everybody loves cotton candy. I guess it transports us back to our childhood and fun memories of carnivals and county fairs. So, why not use it as a garnish on a cocktail.

Here are a few options. The easiest (but least rewarding) option is to simply buy pre-made cotton candy from the grocery store. You can place it on top of the drink or

on a skewer rising above the glass.

A second option is to buy a cotton candy machines and make it yourself. This option allows you to control the flavors that go in the confection. You can even make the cotton candy out of a cocktail. To do that, you need to start with a high-sugar-content drink, and let it dry out. Or you can soak granulated sugar with the spirits/liqueurs and let that dry. Either way, you will need to grind it back to a powder (essentially a flavored sugar) before using in the machine as per manufacturer instructions.

If you do not want to invest in a machine, you can make "spun sugar" (as described in the previous section) and achieve a similar, albeit less dense, product.

CRYSTALLIZING

Crystallized fruits (also called candied fruits or *glacé* fruits) have been produced around the world for centuries as a way to preserve the fruit for the winter. This traditional confection can be used as a garnish for our cocktails. At a high level, the way to candy fruit (or spice like ginger) is to soak and simmer the fruit in a syrup. After a while, the water in the fruit will be replaced by the sugar from the syrup. Through this process, most fruits will retain their vibrant color.

1. Cut the fruit into ¼" slices or dice (unless the fruit is small enough, such as grapes).

2. Make a 1:3 syrup (eg: 3 cups water, 1 cup sugar) and bring to a boil in a saucepan.

3. Carefully add the fruit pieces to the saucepan, ensuring they are all covered.

4. Lower the heat, and simmer for 40-50 minutes, turning the fruits occasionally. Keep an eye on the pan as sugar can boil over. To avoid this, use a pan big enough to hold 3 times the amount of syrup.

5. When done, the fruit will be translucent but remain in one piece.

6. Remove the fruit from the syrup using tongs or a slotted spoon, and cool on a wire rack with

parchment paper underneath to catch drips. Be sure to separate individual pieces so they do not stick together.

7. Let dry overnight.
8. Place fruit in a ziplock bag and add granulated sugar and shake the bag.
9. Store in an airtight container separating the fruits with wax paper (they will keep in the fridge for 6 months).
10. Don't discard the syrup, use it in place of simple syrup in future cocktails.

Here's an example of crystallized ginger served on a cocktail stick.

CANDIED CITRUS PEEL

Candied citrus peel offers a sharp sweet tartness that adds a nice burst of flavors to your drinks.

1. Wash fruit and dry fully.
2. Using a vegetable peeler, cut a swath from the citrus skin.
3. Lay skin flat on a board, pith side up and slice off excess pith (see tips on page 23).
4. Cut the skin into thin strips.
5. Make a simple syrup by boiling equal part of sugar and water (about 1 cup of each for each whole fruit used) for a couple of minutes.
6. Add citrus strips to the boiling syrup. Be careful not to splatter syrup as you add the strips.
7. Reduce heat to low and simmer for 10-12 minutes (the peel will be translucent when done). Be sure to keep an eye on the pan as the sugar can boil over.
8. Remove the strips with a slotted spoon and place in a sieve over parchment paper to drain. Make sure you separate individual pieces so they do not stick to each other.
9. Place the strips in a ziplock bag, add granulated sugar, seal and shake the bag.
10. Remove the strips from the bag and set to dry on waxed paper.
11. Don't discard the syrup, use it in place of simple syrup in future cocktails.

MERINGUE

Meringues are another cool sugary treat you can use to decorate a cocktail. You can simply float one on top of the drink. Don't worry about it getting soggy; even though, over time, it will melt a bit from the contact

with the liquid, during the time it takes to consume the drink, it will retain its shape nicely. You can also hang it on a skewer sticking out of the drink (and even caramelize it at the last minute in front of your guest).

Meringues can be bought at the grocery store, but it's very easy to make your own. And if you do, you'll be able to add flavoring and/or coloring to better match your drink.

Here's the recipe:

1. Preheat oven to 200°F.
2. Line a baking pan with parchment paper.
3. Beat 3 large egg whites and ¼ teaspoon of cream of tartar with a stand or hand-held mixer, on medium speed, until fluffy.
4. Increase the mixer speed to high, and slowly add ¾ cup granulated sugar. Beat until stiff and glossy. Do not overwhip or it will dry up.
5. Pipe (using a pastry bag) or spoon the meringue in 1 ½" mounds on the parchment paper; leave enough space between the mounds so they do not touch when they expand.
6. Bake until crisp and slightly brown (about 1 ½ hours).
7. Let cool fully.
8. Optionally, you can use a small propane torch to caramelize the surface of the meringue.

9. Serve or keep in an airtight container for up to a week.

Chapter 10 – Chocolate

In this chapter, we cover the use of chocolate to create garnishes. Chocolate is the obvious garnish choice for drinks with strong chocolate flavors (for instance those based on crème de cacao), but also those based on coffee flavors (eg: Kalhua, Tia Maria, etc)

You will learn how to temper the chocolate and make various decorative items such as shavings, piping, cutouts, shards, curls, cages, spirals, rims and truffles.

TEMPERING

In order for the chocolate to have the desired glossy appearance, hardness and brittleness and be more resistant to warmer temperatures, it needs to be tempered. Without first tempering the chocolate, you risk the chance that your garnish will melt and lose its shape. This is because cocoa butter consists of different fat groups with different melting points. Those fats that melt at the higher temperature are also the first ones to solidify as the chocolate cools. The tempering process distributes these fats around, and creates the crystalline structure giving chocolate its gloss and hardness. There are a couple of methods to temper the chocolate, both involving melting, cooling and rewarming.

Table Method

1. Cut the chocolate into small pieces, and place in a bowl.
2. Place over a pan of hot water, creating a double-boiler (ensure the water isn't too hot, 140°F is ideal).
3. Stir constantly until the chocolate is all melted and has a temperature of about 120°F.
4. Remove from heat.
5. Take two thirds of the melted chocolate and place on a marble slab.
6. Using a metal scrapper, spread the chocolate, then scrape it back together.
7. Continue doing this until the chocolate has cooled to about 80°F. At this point, it will start thickening (a sign that the high-melting-point fats are crystallizing).
8. Pour the chocolate back into the remaining chocolate and stir until smooth. It will be thick at this point.
9. Put the bowl back over the hot water bath until the temperature reaches about 85-90°F (closer to 85 for milk and white chocolate). This is the correct working temperature.
10. Use the chocolate as instructed.

Seeding Method

1. Follow steps 1-4 of the table method.
2. Slowly add grated chocolate to the melted chocolate (ratio of 1 part grated to 3 parts melted). Stir thoroughly between each addition.

3. When the temperature has dropped to 80°F, stir for for about 2 more minutes.
4. Increase the temperature to 85-90°F (closer to 85° for milk and white chocolate).
5. Use the chocolate as instructed to make the garnishes.

SHAVINGS

The easiest way to use chocolate as a garnish is to simply shred it or shave it over the drink. You don't need to temper the chocolate first. Spread the shavings randomly or use a template to create a specific pattern (see chapter 12 for details on creating a stencil for this purpose).

To create the shavings, hold a small knife at 90 degrees to a block of chocolate, and scrape away from you (place a piece of paper on the table to catch the shavings). Alternatively, use a cheese grater. To create longer shavings, use the same technique with a melon baller instead of a knife.

Store the shavings in a dry cool place until ready to use. To serve, use a cold spoon instead of your hands to avoid melting the chocolate.

SHARDS AND CUTOUTS

Another simple way to decorate a drink is to cut a shape out of a chocolate sheet. You can keep the shape rough for an abstract look (what I call a shard), or you can cut it precisely into a rectangle, triangle, etc. In terms of placement on the cocktail, you can lay it on top or dip it in.

1. Place baking paper on a table.
2. Using a palette knife, spread the tempered chocolate over the paper in a 1/16" layer.
3. Lift the paper and place on a cutting board.

4. Allow the chocolate to set (without refrigerating).
5. Using a knife or pizza cutter, cut the chocolate in the desired shape (don't cut through the paper).
6. Store in a cool dark place (not the fridge).
7. When ready to use, lift the piece while pushing under the paper with your other hand.
8. Place on or in drink.

Variation: marbleized chocolate

For an interesting variation, use both dark and white chocolate, swirled together to create a marble effect.

1. Temper dark and white chocolate (separately). You will need about 2-3 times less white than dark.
2. Place a sheet of parchment paper on a large cutting board.
3. Spread the dark chocolate over the paper in a 1/16" layer.
4. Place the white chocolate in a pastry bag with a small opening.
5. Pipe zigzags of white chocolate in both directions over the dark chocolate.
6. Run a skewer through the chocolate in a circular motion (do not let the skewer touch the paper beneath).
7. Continue swirling until the two colors are mixed in a marbleized fashion.
8. Let cool and use as described above.

CURLS

This technique produces cylinders of chocolate, which can then be dipped in the drink or placed across the top of the glass. This garnish is inspired by the pastry world which uses these curls to decorate the top of cakes.

1. Make sure the room is at the ideal temperature (68°F is about right).
2. Place melted chocolate (not necessarily tempered) over a marble or smooth wood surface (avoid chopping boards, as bits of wood may get into the product).
3. Using a palette knife, spread the chocolate to a thickness of 1/16".
4. Once the melted chocolate has set, use a knife to cut a strip of the desired width.
5. Hold a chef knife or metal pastry scraper at a 45 degrees angle, and push it across the surface away from you to create a 1" curl.

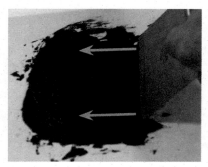

6. Place curl over the drink

This technique takes a bit of practice; so be patient with yourself the first time you try it.

PIPING

Chocolate can be piped in a variety of shapes, that can be laid across the top of the glass, plunged in the drink, stuck in whipped cream and even dangled from the rim. Here are a few of examples:

You can use melted coating chocolate or tempered chocolate. But you need to add a little simple syrup to the chocolate (about ¼ to ¾ teaspoon per cup of melted chocolate). The amount will vary based on the brand and type of chocolate; add enough syrup to get soft peaks. Store this mixture covered in a cool place and melt over a double-boiler when ready to use.

You can use a disposable pastry bag, but if you don't have one, here's how to make a paper piping bag:

1. Cut baking paper into an 8" square.
2. Cut diagonally to make 2 triangles.
3. Hold the 2 points of the long side of the triangle, and fold them over each other to make a cone (the center of the long side becomes the tip of the cone).
4. Fold the top of the cone down to secure the assembly.

Tip

And here's how to create the piped shapes:

1. Prepare piping chocolate as described above.
2. Trace the design you want to create on paper. You can create geometric lines, squiggles, hearts, or even write something (as in the example below).
3. Attach the paper to a piece of cardboard, and attach some baking paper over your drawing.
4. Fill the piping bag halfway with piping chocolate, and fold the bag over to close it.
5. Cut a small opening at the tip of the bag.
6. Pipe the chocolate following the lines of your design. Try to do it in one smooth motion instead of stopping and starting again.
7. Let the chocolate harden and store in a dark cool place (still attached to the paper).
8. When ready to use, place one hand under the paper, and push gently while the other hand carefully picks up the garnish.
9. Place on/in the cocktail as desired.

SPIRAL

Using piping chocolate and a piping bag (as described above), pipe chocolate in a spiral shape inside a martini glass. Place in the freezer until ready to serve. Pour cocktail in the glass.

CAGE

The cage is a delicate but impressive garnish that lays on top of the glass. It is similar to the sugar cage described in chapter 9 but made out of chocolate. They are formed by piping chocolate over a balloon.

1. Prepare piping chocolate as described above.
2. Set a rocks glass on a table nearby.
3. Blow up a small balloon to the desired size and tie the end to secure it.
4. Spread vegetable oil over the balloon.
5. Make a piping bag and fill with piping chocolate (see previous section).
6. Hold the balloon in one hand and piping bag in the other.
7. Pipe chocolate lines covering the balloon to its widest point. Do not make too tight a pattern; you should be able to see through the chocolate lattice and have enough room to put a straw through.
8. Place the balloon on the rocks glass, and put in the refrigerator for a few minutes.
9. Using a needle, poke a small hole in the balloon close to the knot.
10. Put the glass and balloon back in the fridge. The balloon will deflate slowly and eventually fall into the glass, leaving the chocolate cage on top.
11. Remove the cage and place on a pan in the fridge.
12. When ready to use, pour your cocktail, place a cage over the glass and stick a straw through the cage.

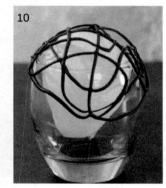

TRUFFLE SKEWER

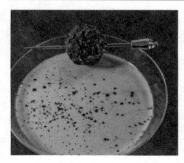

Another cool idea is to skewer a truffle and lay it on the drink. This is a pretty decadent garnish, but goes well with a chocolate martini or other chocolate-flavored after-dinner drinks.

There are many recipes for truffles. Here's a simple one for dark truffles. Feel free to adjust flavors to your liking (for example adding a bit of orange liqueur).

Ingredients (makes about 30 truffles)
- ½ cup heavy cream
- ¼ teaspoon vanilla extract
- 9 ounces sweet dark chocolate, chopped
- 1 ½ ounces soft unsalted butter
- Cocoa powder

Steps
1. Heat cream and vanilla and bring to a boil.
2. Remove from heat and add chocolate.
3. Mix until smooth and the mixture has cooled (to about 85°F).
4. Stir in the butter.
5. Let sit until the mixture is thick.
6. Using a spoon, take some chocolate (about a cherry size worth) and roll in your hands to form a ball.
7. Roll the balls in cocoa powder. You can also dip them in chocolate, drizzle chocolate over them and/or rolled them in nuts.
8. To serve, skewer a truffle and place on top of the drink.

RIM

The rim of the glass can be decorated with chocolate. Please refer to chapter 7 for instructions.

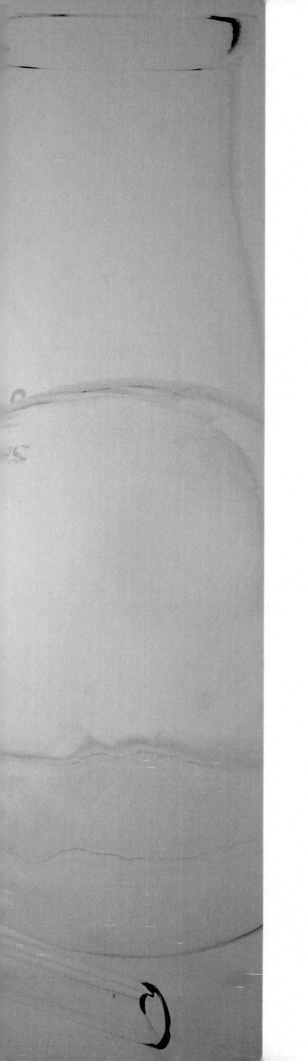

Chapter 11 – Modernist Techniques

The *avant-garde* of the mixology world have started using techniques borrowed from the modernist cuisine and molecular gastronomy movements to create or decorate cocktails. Molecular gastronomy itself is fairly recent, and its concepts were pioneered by such visionaries as Heston Blumenthal (of the Fat Duck in England) and Ferran Adrià (of El Bulli, in Spain).

The techniques are not necessarily difficult to master, but do require some specialized products and/or equipment. These products let you, for instance, turn liquids into gels, spheres, powders and other interesting shapes.

In this section, we will not cover all techniques used in molecular mixology, but only those that have applications as garnishes or provide interesting and non-conventional ways to present cocktails. We will discuss the ingredients and equipment needed, the techniques involved and also give examples of how these can be used to decorate your drinks.

SPHERIFICATION

Spherification is a technique invented by chef Ferran Adrià in 2003. It involves turning a liquid into spheres of various sizes. The spheres are not hard and retain a soft texture. They are essentially a membrane filled with liquid. The most common use of these techniques is in making little balls usually called "caviar". They can be made out of most liquids by mixing the right chemical components, as we will describe later.

Larger items (sometimes called ravioli) can also be made. These are basically a bigger version of the caviar balls but, due to gravity, they tend to not stay perfectly round (they take a shape closer to that of an egg yolk).

At a high level, the techniques involve mixing the liquid with chemical compounds and dripping droplets into a specially-prepared bath. There are two main techniques for spherification: direct and reverse.

Direct Spherification

Direct (also called basic) spherification is the most common of the two methods. In order to use this technique, you will need sodium alginate and calcium salts. Don't let the chemical names scare you. These compounds are perfectly safe for human consumption and can be bought from specialty shops. You can use almost any liquid as the base, except those that contain calcium (such as dairy products), and those that are very acidic (the pH needs to be above 3.6). These limitations reduce the versatility of this method.

The resulting spheres have a very thin membrane around them, which "explodes" in your mouth releasing the flavor. The spheres produced also tend to be more round than with the reverse method described later. On the downside, they are more fragile and need to be handled with care. Finally, they need to be used immediately and do not lend themselves to advanced preparation.

Here are the steps for direct spherification:

1. ***Prepare the liquid to be turned into spheres:***
   a) Prepare the liquid as normal (it could be simply a juice, a puree or a mix of liquids).
   - The liquid should be cold before mixing (otherwise you may get lumps).
   - If the mix is to contain alcohol, it is best to mix sodium alginate with non-alcoholic liquid or water first, as described below, before adding the alcohol.

   b) Thoroughly mix the liquid with sodium alginate at a 0.5% ratio (ie 1g of sodium alginate for each 200g of liquid), using a blender or immersion blender. Make sure the alginate is completely dissolved. It may take several minutes.
   - If the liquid is very watery, it is best to mix the alginate with half of the liquid and use an immersion blender to disperse it (it will be sticky at this point), then add the rest of the liquid.
   - If, on the other hand, the liquid is thick (like a puree), it is best to immersion blend it first with distilled water to achieve a more liquid consistency, then add the main ingredient. It's also a good idea to strain out any pips or fibrous bits, otherwise these may end up clogging your device in step 4.

   c) Let the mix rest in the fridge for at least an hour. This will help remove the bubbles that may have been created in the blending process, thereby ensuring a more uniform end product.

2. ***Prepare the bath:*** in a large bowl, mix calcium salts with distilled water, stirring by hand or using an immersion blender. The ratio is different based on the type of calcium salt used:
   - *Calcium chloride*: 1g for each 200ml of water.
   - *Calcium lactate*: 1 g for each 100ml of water.
   - *Calcium lactate gluconate*: 1g for each 50ml of water. This is my preference as it does not affect flavor.

3. ***Prepare another large bowl with distilled water.***

4. ***Create the caviar spheres:***
   You will need either a large syringe or a so-called caviar maker, which is a special device designed to create a large number of droplets in one shot; essentially, it's a set of pipettes to which you attach a

syringe to pull liquid in. The caviar maker is a much more efficient way to create spheres.

a) Plunge the syringe or caviar maker pipettes in the sodium alginate liquid, and pull to fill with liquid.

b) Hold about 3" over the calcium bath.

c) Push the syringe slowly to release drops of liquid. When the liquid hits the bath, the sodium alginate reacts with the calcium to instantly form a membrane on the outside of the drop. This is what allows the liquid to retain its shape.

d) Lightly stir the bath to keep the spheres moving (without actually touching them) for about a minute. Note that if you wait longer, the membrane will be thicker, which means the spheres will be more sturdy but also less palatable. It's a balancing act, and with practice you will learn what the right consistency needs to be.

e) Using a slotted spoon, remove the spheres from the calcium bath, and place them in the distilled water bowl to rinse them.

5. Serve immediately as the spheres will continue thickening, to the point where they eventually turn into solid (and unpalatable) balls.

Note

Try to keep the bath clean by removing small floating particles from the previous batch that may stick to the new spheres.

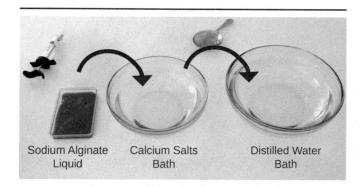

| Sodium Alginate Liquid | Calcium Salts Bath | Distilled Water Bath |

Making Larger Spheres

Follow the steps above, but in step 4.c., instead of using a caviar maker or syringe, spoon (I prefer a spherical measuring spoon) some liquid, and carefully lower it into the bath. You will need to wait longer (about 2 minutes). Make sure to clean your spoon between each pour.

Reverse Spherification

This is essentially the same procedure as the direct method, but this time, we are mixing the calcium in our flavored liquid and making a bath with the sodium alginate. Calcium Lactate Gluconate is usually the salt of choice for this method. One issue with this technique is that the spheres tend to stick together, so we need to ensure they don't touch. This is fairly easy to achieve with large spheres, but with caviar it's almost impossible to prevent them from touching. For this reason, we will describe here only the process for large ravioli-like spheres and not caviar.

This method does not have the constraint of the direct method regarding calcium content or acidity of the base liquid, so it's a bit more versatile. It also produces spheres that are less delicate and require less careful handling. The downside of this technique is that the membrane is thicker, which some people dislike. It also takes longer, since the bath needs to rest for 24 hours; however, with a bit of advanced planning, this may not be that big of an issue. Finally, the spheres tend to be less perfectly round than with the direct method. The steps are as follows:

1. Prepare the liquid to be turned into spheres

a) If the liquid is already high in calcium (for instance, if it based on cream or milk), you probably don't need to add any calcium, though you may need to thin out the liquid if it is too thick.

b) If the liquid does not contain calcium, mix it with calcium lactate gluconate at a ratio of 2% (ie 1g for each 50g of liquid). Mix a third of the liquid with the calcium using an immersion blender. When fully dispersed, add the remainder of the liquid.

c) The thickness of the liquid needs to be neither too watery (otherwise the spheres won't form), nor too thick (or the shape will not be round). After some practice, you will be able to tell the right consistency. If you need to thicken the liquid, you can add xanthan gum (at a ratio of 0.2-0.5%).

d) Let the mixture rest in the fridge for a couple of hours. This will help remove the bubbles that may have been created in the blending process, thereby ensuring a more uniform end product.

2. Prepare the sodium alginate bath:

a) Mix sodium alginate into distilled water at a ratio of 0.5% (ie 1g per 200ml of water), and blend thoroughly using a blender or immersion blender. It make take a few minutes.

b) Pour in a large flat-bottom bowl or pan.

c) Let the bath rest in the refrigerator for 24 hours (to eliminate bubbles).

3. Prepare another large bowl with distilled water.

4. Create the spheres:

a) Spoon the calcium-based liquid. I find using a deep spherical measuring spoon works well, but feel free to experiment with other implements.

b) Gently lower into the bath. Make sure you clean your spoon between each pour.

c) Lightly stir the bath. If you put several spheres in the bath at the same time, make sure they do not come in contact with each other, otherwise they

will stick together. This is the reason for the flat-bottom pan; it makes it easier for them to stay apart and not congregate at the bottom of a round bowl. Also, make sure the spheres stay submerged in the bath and do not float (otherwise the top will not gel properly).

d) Using a slotted spoon, remove the spheres from the sodium alginate bath, and put them in the distilled water bowl to rinse them (1 minute or so).

5. Serve or store. Note that there is less of a time constraint with the reverse method; because the sodium alginate is not in the sphere, they will not continue to solidify once taken out the bath. That being said, if left uncovered they will dry out. So, it is best to store them in the base liquid that was used to make the spheres.

Note

Try to keep the bath clean by removing small floating particles from the previous batch that may stick to the new spheres.

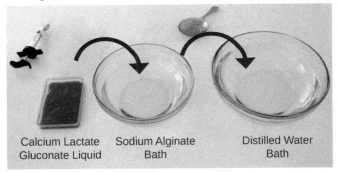

Calcium Lactate   Sodium Alginate   Distilled Water
Gluconate Liquid   Bath   Bath

Tips

- These techniques are not difficult but do require some practice. Do not get discouraged if your first attempts do not turn out perfectly. In particular, you may need to experiment with the thickness of the liquids, since that influences how the spheres form.
- Practice how you pour the liquid and from what height (too high and the spheres will flatten).
- I've shown two size of spheres (small and large) but you can create any size in between by using different size spoons to pour the liquid (see for instance the first picture in this section).
- Remember to be precise in your measurements. A high-precision scale (with 0.1g increments) is an essential tool to make sure you have the right concentration of products.

Using Spheres as Garnishes

Caviar spheres can be dropped/floated into a drink to create an interesting in-the-glass garnish. If the glass is topped with crushed ice, they can also be placed on top of the drink. In this case, I recommend serving the drink with a small spoon, so that the guest can pick them up and eat them along with the drink.

You can also place the caviar spheres in a spoon or other small receptacle placed on top of the drink as a complement to the main drink (see also for instance the ice bowl in chapter 8).

Larger spheres can be dropped/floated into a glass. Depending on the densities, you may even be able to have it float midway (think lava lamp), but it's tricky to get the densities just right.

It goes without saying that the flavor of the spheres should complement the drink either by using similar ingredients or providing an interesting contrast.

Finally, you could make the spheres themselves the main attraction. You can turn a cocktail into caviar and serve in a cup with a spoon or serve a larger ravioli on a plate.

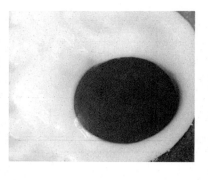

As another example, take a look at my fried egg rendition made with a mangorum sphere (using the reverse spherification method) served on a coconut milk "white" created with agar-agar (a vegetarian substitute for gelatin).

FOAMS

Foams are not a new concept. They have been used for a long time in cooking and desserts. After all, ice-creams, mousses, meringues and cakes are all based on foams. Eggs and cream are two common ingredients that have been used to create foams. But, by using certain chemical ingredients, modernist chefs have expanded the realm of possibilities.

In its most basic definition, a foam is simply air (or a gas) suspended in a liquid or solid. In order for the surface tension of a liquid to be high enough to contain a gas for a significant period of time, there needs to be an emulsifier involved. Emulsifiers help to bind molecules of ingredients that would normally not mix (think of the soap in your bubble bath, which allows the suds to form).

There are many types of foams from meringues to baked goods, mousses and others. But, since this is a book on cocktail garnishes, I will limit this discussion to those foams that can be used as such.

Keep in mind that alcohol does not foam well. So, avoid strong spirits and limit yourself to low-alcohol ingredients such as wine. Also, avoid adding too much acid to the foam, otherwise it may break.

Egg White Foams

The easiest and most common way to create a foam on a cocktail is by using an egg white. The white is added to the shaker, along with the other ingredients. The drink is then first "dry shaken", which means it is shaken without ice. Then it is shaken with ice as usual, before being strained and poured into the serving glass. The foam – being lighter than the liquid – floats to the top creating a nice creamy topping for the drink.

The reason this technique works is that the protein in the egg white acts as the emulsifier, providing the surface tension for the liquid to trap small bubbles of air.

When dry shaking, pay attention to the seal between the two parts of the shaker. Since no ice is involved, the usual vacuum seal present when shaking cocktails will not happen.

So be careful to keep the two parts together, or you may end up with an egg-white-coated guest...

As an example, here's the recipe for a Pisco Sour, a classic egg-white-based cocktail from Peru.

Ingredients

- 1 ½ ounces Pisco
- 1 ounce lime juice
- ¾ ounce simple syrup
- 1 egg white
- Angostura bitters

Steps

1. Add all ingredients (except bitters) to a shaker and dry shake (i.e. without ice).
2. Add ice and shake again.
3. Strain into an old-fashioned glass.
4. Place a few drops of bitters on top of the drink, and optionally run a skewer through them to create a pattern (see chapter 12 for details on creating such patterns).

Flips

Flips follow a similar process as described above, but use a whole egg instead of just the white. The yolk contributes lecithin (a good emulsifier), which adds to the protein network created by the white.

Fizzes

Fizzes are another category of drinks in the same vein as the ones above. They also use egg whites (and sometimes whole eggs), and follow a similar process as the sour, but they are topped with soda water.

Whipped Cream Foams

Cream is the other commonly-used ingredient to create foams: simply flavor the cream as desired, then whip it. The whipped cream can then be spooned, piped (using a pastry bag) or dispensed out of a whipper onto the top of the drink. Here are a few ways to whip the cream:

Using a manual whisk

This is obviously the most traditional, but also most labor-intensive method to whip cream.

Using a hand-held or stand mixer

Also a commonly accepted method, where the machine does the whipping for you.

Using an immersion blender or whipping wand

These create light, frothy foams, like those found on top of lattes.

Using a cream whipper (also called "siphon")

This is, in my opinion, the best way to create foams. It does require purchasing a new device, but this is a very versatile tool. Beside whipping cream, you can use it to carbonate beverages and infuse flavors into spirits in record times.

For the foam to work, the ingredients need to have a high fat content. For items that are fat-free, you need to add gelatin (½ to ¾ teaspoon) or agar-agar (¼ to ½ teaspoon).

The whipper takes the form of a canister with a siphon and a gas cartridge holder. To use it, you:

1. Pour your ingredients into the canister (up to the maximum specified by the manufacturer).
2. Close the device.
3. Shake.
4. Load a cartridge or two of compressed gas (nitrous oxide or carbon dioxide) to pressurize the device.
5. Shake again and refrigerate.
6. When ready to use, shake a bit more, turn whipper upside down, aim over the drink, and push the trigger to release the foam. Alternatively, you can dispense the foam at the bottom of the glass, and pour the drink on top (the foam will float up to the top).

Tips

- Make sure you strain your ingredients, otherwise chunks may clog the device.
- Choose the ingredients of the foam such that they stand on their own but also go well with the drink the foam will be topping.
- Instead of gelatin (or agar-agar), you can also use egg whites to create structure. In this case, add some lemon juice (to break the bond) and sugar (to stabilize the bond).

Here's an example of creating a liqueur-and-wine-based foam using a cream whipper.

Ingredients

- 3 ½ ounces low-alcohol liqueur (eg: St Germain).
- 3 ½ ounces white wine
- 2g gelatin (substitute agar-agar if you're vegetarian)

Steps

1. Pour liqueur and wine in a saucepan, and warm on medium heat.
2. Stir in gelatin or agar-agar, and dissolve fully.
3. Remove from heat and let cool.
4. Pour into a cream whipper, shake and charge with 2 gas cartridges per manufacturer's instructions.
5. Shake canister again.
6. Refrigerate for at least an hour.
7. Before serving, shake again and dispense on top the drink.

Gum-based Foams

Thickeners such as xanthan gum, guar gum and locust bean gum can be used to help create foams. Bubbles will form naturally in liquids, but usually will not last. For instance, when rapidly pouring a glass of water from a faucet, you will sometimes see bubbles form but only briefly. These thickeners will help create a more stable foam, but they usually need to be used in combination with emulsifiers for better results.

Gelling agents

Gelatin can be used to create foams, but unfortunately the foam will not remain stable at room temperature. Agar-agar is a jelly-like substance obtained from algae and has gelling properties. Beside being acceptable to vegetarians, it also has the advantage of being stable at room temperature. Therefore, it is a better choice than gelatin to create foams.

Versawhip

Versawhip is another good option to create foams. It is a commercial product with a proprietary formula, but it is stronger than egg white and has a wider temperature range than gelatin. It works well with acidic products but not with fatty ones.

To use it, have your liquid ingredients in a running stand mixer, and sprinkle the Versawhip powder in it (typical ratio is 0.5% to 2.0% by weight). Then refrigerate for a few hours. The resulting foam will be airy (at low concentrations) or creamy (at higher concentrations). Xanthan gum (at 0.1% to 0.2%) can be added for a denser and more stable product.

Airs and Espumas

Airs and espumas (which means foam in Spanish) are very light foams, concentrating flavors without any substantive texture. Adding an air on top of a cocktail is a nice-looking and elegant way to introduce a flavor to the drink while decorating it. The guest will taste the flavor of the air as he/she sips the drink, but will not feel any texture change.

Lecithin is a common ingredient used to make airs. To create the air, add lecithin (at a 0.3% to 1% ratio by weight) to the liquid and mix thoroughly with an immersion blender (about 60 seconds to a few minutes). Bubbles will form on top. Let the foam stabilize for a minute, then spoon the bubbles onto the drink. Depending on the liquid, the foam will remain stable for 30 minutes to a couple of hours, but it will deteriorate slightly over time, so it's best to use it soon after making.

Lecithin will work well with most liquids (including acidic ones), but keep in mind that the flavors will be diluted as air is whipped in, so start with a very flavorful liquid.

Another method involves using a fish tank air pump. In order to use this method, prepare a liquid that has a good level of viscosity (you may need to use an agent such as xanthan gum or Versawhip). Plunge the tube of the fish tank pump into the liquid, and start the pump. This will form very large bubbles, which can then be scooped and placed on top of the drink.

A good example of using an air as a garnish is the salt air margarita popularized by José Andrés. Instead of using salt on the rim, you can make a salt air, which will give the guest a nice hit of salt with each sip. To create this air, combine 4 ounces of water, 2  ounces of fresh lime juice, 1 ½ teaspoons of sucrose esters (such as Sucro) and 1 ½ teaspoons of salt in a bowl, and mix with an immersion blender until bubbles form. You can then scoop the bubbles on top of the margarita.

PAPER COCKTAILS

This techniques, introduced by Eben Freeman, results in a very thin translucent solid sheet of cocktail. You can place this "paper" on top of the glass for an unconventional garnish. You can use the same recipe as the drink itself, or make it an interesting complement. Keep in mind that whatever you use to make the paper will need to have very strong flavors, otherwise the paper will be flavorless. It's also recommended to use a colorful beverage otherwise the final product will look bland.

Here's the procedure. You will need some square (or round) thin edible films; these can be bought from stores specializing in molecular gastronomy ingredients. The finished sheets can be kept in an airtight container separated by parchment paper. But be careful as they are very fragile.

1. Cut edible films to the size and shape you want (in the example below, I used half-circles).
2. Prepare the cocktail to be used as a base (make sure it's a strong flavor) and place in a spray bottle.
3. Place parchment paper on a dehydrator tray.
4. Spray cocktail on parchment paper (about the size of the edible film).
5. Place one edible film on top of the sprayed cocktail.
6. Spray more cocktail on the edible film.
7. Place a second edible film on top of the first, lining up the edges.
8. Spray more cocktail on the edible film.
9. Repeat with 2 more layers of edible film and cocktail spray.
10. Give the assembly one final spray. Don't worry if the color is not even. Personally, I actually prefer an uneven, marbleized look.
11. You can optionally sprinkle small flavoring bits (such a shavings of orange peels) at this stage.
12. Put tray in a dehydrator at 125°F. If you do not have a dehydrator, use a low temperature oven.
13. Dehydrate until the sheets are dry and crispy. This may take several hours depending on your dehydrator or oven.
14. Remove the films from the parchment paper.
15. Balance the cocktail paper on top of the glass.

POWDERED COCKTAILS

Serving a cocktail as a powder may not be everybody's idea of a good time, but it definitely makes for an interesting conversation piece. Modernist chefs have been turning liquids into powders for some time now with creations such as olive oil powder and other similarly disconcerting items. In the cocktail world, some bartenders have turned liqueurs to powder and used them to rim a glass (as illustrated below) or as a sprinkle over a frothy drink.

The key ingredient to accomplish this feat is tapioca maltodextrin (N-Zorbit is a good example). This modified starch's granules have a texture such that they absorb liquid very well.

1. Mix 3 ½ ounces of tapioca maltodextrin with one ounce of liquid.
2. Stir thoroughly until dry. You may need to add more maltodextrin if it's still moist.
3. Sift through a sieve to create a nice powder.
4. Serve by itself as a novelty item or as an accompaniment for another cocktail (on a rim or as a sprinkle).

A simpler method is to slowly dehydrate the liqueur (in a dehydrator or very low oven) and grind it to a powder using a mortar and pestle (see chapter 7 for details). But the alcohol evaporates in the process, so you are not really left with powdered cocktail, but simply sugar and a powdery residue with the flavors that were in the original product. Still usable, but missing the alcohol component. Also, this method does not seem to work consistently; some liqueurs crystallize, some don't, depending on the sugar content (Campari and Chartreuse seem to work well).

Suspending in Liquid

Another stunning presentation invented by Ferran Adrià involves suspending fruits in liquid. He used this technique to create a white sangria with herbs, fruits and caviar spheres (see spherification section).

In order for the fruits to stay level, you need to thicken the liquid with xanthan gum (0.3% ratio), stirring with an immersion blender and refrigerate for a few hours. When you get ready to serve it, pour the thickened liquid in the glass, then arrange the bits of fruit and herbs at different levels. Serve with a spoon.

they both contain *mehtyl hexanoate*.

Of course, some of these theoretical pairings don't really pan out in practice. So experiment. For more information on this type of pairings, check out foodpairing.com.

Eat-and-Drink Cocktails

Another trend in the modernist movement is to serve a bite of food with the cocktail, sometimes placed near the drink, sometimes perched on top. The food is expected to complement the drink's flavors of course. But the pairing is not always obvious and can sometimes seem downright weird. This is because these pairings are often based on matching foods that have common molecular compounds.

Our perception of food is only based 20% on taste, and the vast majority of what we call "taste" actually comes from aromas (i.e. the smell). With that in mind, scientists have been putting together aroma profiles for each food and drink. Then based on commonalities, pairings are determined. Some are intuitive (like chocolate and strawberry), but the analysis sometimes uncovers combinations that nobody would think would work. For example, pineapple pairs well with blue cheese, because

Smoke

Smoke has been used for centuries to impart flavors to meats and other dishes. But it's only recently that bartenders have started actively using smoke in their creations. Of course, smoky flavors in spirits are not new: liquors like scotch or mezcal already have a built-in smoky flavor due to their manufacturing process.

But there's now a new trend to add smoke to drinks using a portable tool (such as the Smoking Gun) that burns wood chips and produces smoke. The typical procedure involves piping smoke from the tool to a bottle, then adding the drink to

the bottle and shaking a few times (being careful not to over-smoke).

Smoke can also be created by using dry ice. For instance, by mixing dry ice with a chocolate liqueur in a small receptacle, you can create a chocolate smoke that permeates the air. Do not serve the dry ice to the guest; use it only to create the smell.

In terms of garnishing, we can use smoke (to add visual appeal to our cocktails. Here are a few ideas:

- Leave a gap at the top of the glass, pipe some smoke in and top with a coaster. Serve with the coaster on so that the smoke disperses as the guest removes it, thereby generating aroma and visual drama.

- Fill a balloon with perfumed smoke, and attach the balloon to the stem of the glass. Then burst the balloon when serving to release the smell.

- Create a flavored smoke, and serve the cocktail under a glass dome filled with that smoke. As the dome is lifted in front of the guest, the aroma will provide an extra dimension of experience.

- Serve the cocktail in a small bottle with smoke added on top. The guest then pours the drink from the bottle into the glass getting a whiff of smoke in the process. Also, if some of the drink is left in the bottle longer, it will gradually pick up more smoke flavor, creating an evolving drink.

Chapter 12 – Miscellaneous Garnishes

This chapter contains a few more interesting garnish techniques that did not fit cleanly in any other category.

We first discuss how to decorate the top of frothy or creamy cocktails with various patterns. These patterns can be made with bitters, sauces or powdered spices and can be created using stencils or toothpicks.

We also cover the creation and use of dehydrated fruits as garnishes and touch briefly on the idea of using the garnish as the container for the drink.

We conclude the chapter with a discussion on the use of inedible garnishes.

PATTERNS

Patterns can easily be created on the top of frothy or creamy cocktails by dropping some bitters and running a toothpick through the drops to elongate them. This technique is frequently used in coffee shops and in dessert plating. For instance, the pastry chef may have a pool of raspberry coulis on the plate; he will drop a few dots of a contrasting sauce into the coulis using a squeeze bottle, then run a skewer through each dot to create hearts.

We can use the same technique with cocktails. The base is the top of the cocktail, and the contrasting "sauce" is made of bitters.

This will not work well on purely liquid cocktail; in order to be able to "pull" the bitters, the base surface needs to have a sturdy but soft texture. This will be the case for cocktails using egg whites, cream, as well as those topped with a foam. It's also important that the color of the cocktail contrast well with the color of the bitters or sauce you are planning to use.

When using bitters to create patterns, keep in mind that the drink needs to remain balanced. Be careful to not add a lot of bitters just to create an interesting pattern, which could result in a drink that is too bitter.

Bitter Hearts

This design will appear as a series of hearts. They can be arranged in a line or in a circle pattern.

To place the drops of bitters, I find the standard dashers that come on most bitters bottles impractical, as you cannot exactly control where the drops will land. So, I transfer the bitters to a small glass bottle with a dropper top. This way I can place drops exactly where I need them.

1. Prepare a frothy or creamy cocktail as usual.
2. Using a dropper, place several drops of bitters on the surface. They can form a line, a circle or whatever shape you want. It is usually more pleasing to the eye if the number of drops is odd.
3. Drag a toothpick through each drop of bitters. This will pull a little bitter off one side and drag it to the other creating a heart shape.

Napoleon Pattern

This design may be known by a different name, but this is what I call it since it is a common design on traditional French Napoleon cakes. They are basically just lines that are pulled in opposite directions to create alternating curves.

Note that this design requires a lot of bitters (probably too much for most people) so a sauce (such as a coulis or chocolate sauce) tends to work better. In this case, make sure the sauce's density matches that of the cocktail or it will sink to the bottom when piped.

1. Prepare a frothy or creamy cocktail as usual.
2. Draw concentric circles with the sauce (using a squeeze bottle). Try to keep the circles evenly spaced.
3. Drag a toothpick from the center to the edge to pull the lines to a point.
4. Repeat around the drink.

You can pull all the lines in the same direction (from center to edge) or you can alternate the direction (center to edge then edge to center).

The picture above shows a few concentric circles with lines in alternating directions.

The following example illustrates two concentric circles with lines from center to edge.

Variation

Instead of concentric circles, you can draw parallel lines with the sauce. The technique is the same: depending on the effect you want, pull a skewer across the lines in alternating directions (top to bottom then bottom to top) or consistent direction.

Other Dragged Patterns

The two patterns described above are classic examples, but feel free to experiment with different shapes using the same technique of dragging a toothpick across lines of bitters or sauce.

High-end coffee shops can be a good source of inspiration, as they often use similar techniques on lattes.

STENCILS

An easy and cheap way to add an impressive design to the top of the cocktail is to use a stencil, and spray bitters over it. This allows you to create any design, and is therefore less limiting than the dragged patterns described previously. The same warning applies regarding the consistency of the cocktail. You need a sturdy base to spray on. It also needs to be a contrasting color to the bitters you are planning to use.

It takes a bit of time to create the stencil, but it can be reused many times. The stencil needs to be made of food-grade plastic. The easiest and cheapest option is to use the lid of a to-go container. You will also need a small spray bottle to which you transfer your bitters for spraying.

Creating your stencil.

1. Draw or print the image you want to use as your design. Make sure it will fit within the diameter of the glass you are planning to use. Keep the image fairly large and not too detailed, otherwise it might be too difficult to cut and hard to see what it represents on the final product.

2. Tape the image to the back of a transparent to-go container lid (with the image facing up) and place on a cutting board.

3. Using an x-acto knife, cut the plastic following the design.

4. Remove the paper and tape.

5. Smooth out any rough edges.

6. Wash the stencil before use.

Using your stencil

1. Prepare a frothy or creamy cocktail as usual. Make sure it reaches close to the top of the glass. If there's too large a distance between the stencil and the drink, the pattern will not be as sharp.

2. Place the stencil on top the glass.

3. Spray the bitters on the stencil, making sure to cover all the holes in the pattern evenly.

4. Carefully lift the stencil.

Variation

Instead of spraying bitters, you can also sprinkle sifted cocoa powered, cinnamon or other powdered spices. Just make sure their flavor goes with the drink you are stenciling, and ensure you sprinkle evenly.

MARSHMALLOWS

Marshmallows can be used for an unusual garnish. They are a good match for decadent creamy cocktails.

Since they can get soggy easily, it is best to perch them on the rim of the glass or on a stick (as in this example).

Here are a couple of examples of how to garnish with dehydrated fruit: one uses a dried apple slice hanging on the rim, and in the other, dried orange slices (along with a cinnamon stick) decorate a glass of mulled wine.

DEHYDRATED FRUIT

Dehydrated fruit provides a rustic yet elegant option as a cocktail garnish. The most common fruits used for this purpose are citrus, apples and pineapples. It is best to dehydrate fruits when they are in season, as they will be at their best and their cheapest. They store pretty well (as long as they are kept in an airtight container), so if you make enough, you will have them available all year. Note that you can also dry frozen fruit.

The best way to dehydrate fruit is with a food dehydrator. Set the temperature to 125-135°F. Any higher may result in a hard edge. So, don't try to save time by using a higher temperature. If you do not have a food dehydrator, use an oven at 170°F, placing the fruit on a cooling rack on top of a baking sheet.

1. Wash the fruit.
2. Remove the inedible parts if applicable (eg: pits, cores,...)
3. Cut fruit in ⅜" - ¼" thick slices.
4. Fruits such as bananas, apples and strawberries may oxidize and turn an undesirable color, so spray them liberally with lemon juice.
5. Place fruit on the dehydrator's trays.
6. Rotate the trays every 2 hours for even drying.
7. Dying times vary based on the fruit and its size. When done the fruit will be fully dry but still soft (they will harden as they cool). Lime and lemon can take up to 5 hours; oranges up to 7 hours; large citrus like grapefruit up to 9 hours; apples 4-10 hours.
8. Remove from dehydrator or oven and let cool.
9. If you're planning to vacuum-seal the fruit, first place them in a ziplock bag and keep in kitchen for 24 hours (this will help distribute the moisture evenly).

Beside fruits, you can also dehydrate thin slices of lotus root. Their beautiful shape provides a lovely garnish when floated on top of a drink. You can also color them (cooking them in a beet syrup for instance) to provide a better contrast.

Garnish as a Container

Using an interesting vessel to serve the drink can also be considered a garnish. For instance, some tiki mugs are works of art in and of themselves, and they add to the visual appeal of the drink. Another example is to serve the drink in a coconut, bell pepper, pineapple, melon or even a citrus (or any other produce you deem suitable).

Of course, even when the container is decorative, you can add conventional garnishes on top.

Inedible Garnishes

Finally, we conclude this chapter and this book with a mention of inedible garnishes. These have fallen out of favor for the most part and been relegated to the tiki world, where kitsch and cheesy is the name of the game.

Plastic Items

Another common garnish found on tiki drinks are little plastic items; they can take the shape of animals, pirates, swords, etc... and are usually found perched on the drink or dangling from the rim of the glass.

Stir sticks and swizzle sticks also fall under the category of inedible garnishes. Most of the time, they are just functional and not particularly aesthetically pleasing. However, there are a number of "fancy" sticks, where the top is in the shape of a palm tree, a parrot, a flamingo or similar.

Umbrellas

The most ubiquitous of such garnishes is the cocktail umbrella. The origins and purpose of the umbrella are not clear, but the tiki meccas Don the Beach Comber and Trader Vic's are credited with its introduction. Little paper flags are sometimes used as well.

Straws

Straws are mostly utilitarian, but they can also act as a garnish. For instance, there are decorative straws such as the so-called "crazy straws", which have bends and loops at the end. These are a bit garish and are probably only suitable for tropical drinks.

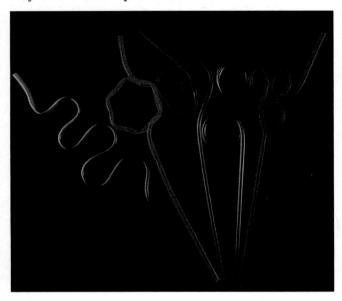

Stainless steel straws can look classy in the right context, though some people dislike the taste and feel of metal as they sip.

Finally, there are a few more exotic options, such as using bamboo and lemongrass (possibly candied) as a straw.

DECORATING THE STEM

Throughout most of this book, we have been discussing garnishes that sit above the drink, on the rim or are plunged in the drink. But we can also add visual appeal to the cocktail by decorating the stem. For instance, you may want to tie a ribbon around it, or perhaps wrap a necklace (or some beads for Mardi Gras).

Epilogue

We've covered a lot of ground in this book. I hope the various techniques we discussed have helped you step up your cocktail garnish game. More importantly, I hope this book will inspire you to come up with your own garnish creations.

I welcome any comment and feedback on this book. Just shoot me an email at philippe@cocktailgarnish.com. Also feel free to send me your cool garnish ideas and I may incorporate them in a future edition of this book.

Good luck and have fun!

Philippe

Made in the USA
Middletown, DE
16 October 2022

12879516R00075